D0775637

Beyond the Horizon

By

Marvin Wilmes

A Memoir

Copyright © 2015 Marvin Wilmes

All rights reserved.

ISBN: **10: 1507607989**
ISBN-13: 978-1507607985

DEDICATION

To all the caregivers of the world who tirelessly answer God's call to service.

ACKNOWLEDGMENTS

To my wife, Lori, who has been the true "wind beneath my wings" in this life. To my father, Alfred, and my siblings, Vincent, David, Dean, Norbert, Linda, Nancy, Roland and Karl who lived this with me. Thanks to Aunt Helen for asking the why not question and Aunt Dee for being the best older "sis" ever. I wish to thank author Jerry Jenkins, the Christian Writers Guild, my mentors Julie Allyson-Ieron and Carolyn Walker, and my editor G. Mikel Hayden for making this book the best it can be by helping me chisel out the story. Finally, a tribute to my late mother, Peggy Wilmes, who gave me the creativity to write this story, and my late mother-in-law, Shirley Chihak who always believed I would do this someday.

CONTENTS

INTRODUCTION

The past is behind you and the future is ahead of you; so push forward and move on with your life.

The sign on the front of the neighborhood church startled me, and I considered the reality that a memoir is all about the past.

At one point in this book's inception, I shelved it because I thought to myself, *Aren't you just stirring up old memories for no real purpose?*

Yet, while attending a 50th wedding anniversary in 2013, witnessing the incredible devotion of my Aunt Donna to my Uncle Joe, who suffered from severe COPD, I recalled a voice from the past.

"If you think this is bad, just wait."

The comment, delivered to me during an intensely trying time in my life, was meant to empathize with what I was feeling at the moment, but my spirit rejected it out of hand.

What this woman meant then, and what those words mean now in hindsight, are two different things. She challenged my entire belief system, and if I hadn't been careful, her words could easily have become a self-fulfilling prophesy.

I've always known that I have something to say. I realized I had to write this book, and when I pulled it off the shelf and began to examine it again, I saw that a story I never believed I could deliver with honesty was staring me in the face.

Blessed are they who mourn, for they shall be comforted. *Matthew 5:. 4*

Are you one who mourns?

Have you experienced a loss that at times seems insurmountable: the loss of a loved one, a cherished dream, a relationship, a job, health or finances?

The purpose of my memoir is not just to tell my story, rather it is to comfort those who mourn and to help them overcome their challenge and move on with their lives. It is to encourage the process of proper grieving, of proper "putting away" and of taking on a powerful force of forgiveness and insight into our purpose in life.

So the church sign and my mission statement are born out of the same well of inspiration.

As I was walking along the Santa Monica beach while vacationing in June of 2014, a seagull flew across the landscape of the horizon.

While I was out on a whale watching tour, the dance of the dolphins was what captivated my attention. I was hardly even disappointed that we didn't see one blue whale.

Water has always provided me with serenity, yet I have always held a healthy respect for it and sometimes an irrational fear of it. The closest I ever came to learning to swim was treading water for three minutes as a Marine Corps recruit in boot camp in 1975.

Having overcome my trepidation and dread of those three minutes, I held onto the side of the pool, hardly believing what I had just done. The drill instructor took hold of my hand and pulled me up and over onto the concrete.

As I reveled in feeling grounded, a whistle sounded calling for all recruits to get out of the pool. I frantically searched for my friend's familiar face. Someone had gone under the water, and I feared for his safety.

My eyes rested on him and I sighed in relief; he wasn't the one in danger—but what had happened to another one of my platoon mates?

My attention was quickly diverted to the large pool as the drill instructor, who'd jumped in to save one of our own burst from beneath the surface with the victim. We all began chattering among ourselves while the drill instructor performed CPR, and my fellow Marine gasped and gurgled, spewing out water and his breakfast from his mouth.

The sight wasn't a pretty one, but a life was saved that day, and my fear of water was ground in even deeper.

So why did the seagull and the ocean have such a perfect message during this California summer sunset?

The sunset outlined the horizon separating the blue sky from the rocks and water, which provided the portrait of serenity that lay before me.

I believe God created a natural process for us all to go through in overcoming life's many challenges. As I am the clay pot that the master potter works with to produce such an imperfect work of art, I am here to share my own story of processing life's events from the scattered remnants of the past into golden truths of the future.

My hope is you will learn, just as I have, that the important things are not what we see directly in the natural realm of this earthly life, but rather what we see in the truth that lies just beyond the horizon.

1 – ALL IN THE FAMILY

As 1963 dawned, the nation was wrapped in a cocoon of innocence.

Life was simple, and my experiences for the first seven years of my life, growing up on a farm in the shadow of my uncles Phil, Tom and Ken, caused me to have a case of "sibling" identification with them.

Uncle Phil was the one who tutored me on the finer points of climbing over a fence when I was a toddler. His strong hands helped me overcome my fear of heights as he encouraged me to take each step up carefully and slowly.

"Come on, Marvin, easy does it," he said. "You've got it."

"Don't let me fall."

Phil chuckled. "Don't worry about that. I'll catch ya."

Uncle Tom was the daredevil. He took me for a ride in his Chevy convertible while the wind blew against my face, and he lit cherry bombs, throwing them out the side of the car.

"Oh yeah," he screamed into the wind as I pushed on the imaginary brakes on my side of the vehicle. All I could do was grin sheepishly, enjoying the thrill of the moment.

I would challenge one of my biggest fears annually by turning on our old Sylvania black-and-white television set in the living room and watching in awe when the Wicked Witch of the West appeared out of a cloud of smoke in the classic *The Wizard of Oz.*

On a Saturday evening as my parents prepared to go out for the night, my uncle Tom came by to babysit my younger brother and me.

"Can we watch the *Wizard of Oz,*" I pleaded.

"I guess so," Tom said, "though I've seen it about a hundred times."

Once the witch appeared on the screen, I fled to my bedroom and climbed under the bed.

Tom followed me into the room, barely able to hide his frustration. "Why are you so scared? You've seen this before? Come on out of there."

"No, I don't like her."

"So why did you want to watch?"

I really didn't know the answer to that question. Fear and things that go bump in the night haunt all young children. Something about the adventure of the imagination made me watch the classic movie over and over, year after year, and cringe in fear at the same time.

My fear of witches came nowhere close to my fear of needles. Our family physician's nurse reminded me of the Wicked Witch of the West every time she gave me a shot.

No matter how brave I tried to be, I always had a bruise to show for it.

That was why when it came time for Aunt Dee and Uncle Ken to go with me to get our smallpox vaccinations, I feared the worst.

"You 'fraidy cat, you ain't gonna be afraid of no needle," Dee, the baby of my father's family, challenged me.

"You have no idea about this nurse," I countered. "She's mean, and her shots always hurt."

Only three years older than I, Dee enjoyed her "big sis" role with me. "I'll get mine first so you can see you have nothing to worry about," Dee offered.

"I'll take you up on that," I said.

When I watched Dee get her smallpox vaccination, I was somewhat encouraged. "Just a pin prick," she declared.

I approached the staid nurse with all the bravery I could muster, lifted the sleeve of my shirt and squeezed my eyes shut as tight as I could while I braced for the pain to come.

"There, all done."

I peeked out of one eye, unsure of my good fortune.

Sure enough, the nurse was smiling, and I wasn't crying.

Roy and Naomi

I was born Marvin LeRoy Wilmes, the third grandchild of George and Gertrude Wilmes who would amaze many a neighbor and friend with their commitment to the Lord's command to be fruitful and multiply.

My father, Alfred Francis Wilmes, was the second oldest of 16 children, and my mother, Margaret Ellen Tuttle Wilmes, was an only child. She had the nickname of "Peggy," which endeared her to many of her closest friends and family.

These contrasts in my parents' family dynamics would enrich my life in a unique way. My father developed a strong work ethic on the farm, and my mother seemed born to nurture.

In all sadness, there is joy; in all joy, there is sadness.

The paradox in this statement, which I heard and hung on to during a crucial turning point in my life, is obvious. How can one find joy in sadness or alternatively sadness in joy?

The latter can best be illustrated through the story of how in 1953, my father sought out my mother's father to honor him with a request for my mother's hand in marriage. In so doing, he would be on his way to becoming the son my grandfather never had.

My mother was the middle child of three and the sole survivor as her brothers had died at childbirth.

My father's confidence and clear purpose for his future life with Roy's daughter was something the elder man could not resist. He gave his blessings, and so began a deep relationship between these two men that lasted many years.

Roy Tuttle's heart was filled with joy that his daughter had found a man to make her dreams come true, but his sadness lay in the reality that he must let his angel go. He must allow her to be free to live her life independent of his dreams for her.

Roy was a quiet man of few words, and his greatest joy was yet to come as a grandfather of nine, a role that would suit him well.

My mother often commented how blessed she was to have so many brothers and sisters after she married my father.

Her mother, Naomi Miller Tuttle, was a schoolteacher by trade. She began her teaching career in the one-room schoolhouses of yesteryear. Teaching came naturally to Mrs. Tuttle, and she could most easily relate to children of school-age years.

Often, my mother would tell stories about how she kept her parents up in the wee hours of every night as she experienced what was diagnosed as colic in her first year.

Did the parents who had experienced the short life of their firstborn retain an anxiety that death might rob them of their dream once again? This past trauma and the death of Peggy's second brother at birth was largely responsible for my grandmother's uncomfortable stance holding a newborn or relating to a toddler.

While during the daughter's school-age years, mother and daughter bonded more deeply, the separation phase when her daughter passed into adulthood became much harder for Naomi to maneuver through. She would always view her only daughter as "her little girl."

Peggy would, herself, learn how to navigate through this phase successfully, however, and Alfred, my father, would help her gain that sense of independence and provide her with the role of farm wife and mother that was her simple dream in life.

Few of her friends and family would recognize her admirable resolve, though this quiet woman of faith would touch many lives in her own passage of time. My mother was very close to both her parents, so close that often she would experience much sadness in that joy.

Grandpa Roy always cast a huge shadow over my life as he was the easygoing one and was always the most comfortable in his grandparent role.

As the oldest of six siblings himself, he experienced many struggles on his way to adulthood. His mother died of tuberculosis when he was just nine years old, and he and four of his siblings went to live with a patriarch, Pat Gorman, and his family.

His youngest sister, Frances, was adopted by another family at the age of six months, something she never knew until decades later, since she was raised as Frances Carroll.

Life for Roy and his siblings would be one of hard work and a loss that Roy never quite understood. His father, Tom Tuttle, abandoned the children shortly after their mother died. Why this occurred and what happened to his father were questions never answered and since such issues were never looked into in his generation, my grandfather assumed the worst-case scenario of desertion.

Roy labored for many years as a hired hand and moved his family from farm to farm, often annually. Naomi worked outside the home as a schoolteacher.

Roy eventually scraped enough money together to buy his own farm and to plant some roots northwest of Parnell, Missouri in the rolling hills of Worth County where Peggy spent her teenage years.

However, Roy could barely keep up with the technological changes in farming, and Naomi decided to obtain her Master's degree in education at the Northwest Missouri State Teacher's College in Maryville.

Upon graduation, Naomi was offered a teaching position in Southeast Elementary School in Kansas City. She was elated at her good fortune, but selling the farm was one of the greatest traumas of her life. My mother often recounted the day's events when she consoled her mother, who couldn't bear the thought of letting go of the farm she and her husband had worked so hard to own.

Roy followed Naomi to the Kansas City area, which was one of the greatest turning points in his life. He initially became a school bus driver and found himself enamored by contact with youth. That experience led him to apply for a position as a custodian for Platte Hills Junior High School, where he found his true destiny as a father figure for many of the young students there.

Roy would work the night shift and Naomi would teach nine months out of the year. The two forged new friendships, and their daughter and her family were only two hours away.

My grandparents often traveled to Nodaway County, and my mother would also make sure we traveled often to Parkville, Missouri. Going to Grandma and Grandpa's house had a special meaning for my brother, Vincent, and me.

For Roy and Naomi Tuttle, the move to the Kansas City, Missouri area meant a new lease on life and financial security that would last to their retirement and beyond.

George and Gertrude

My paternal grandfather was a great storyteller, waving his hand missing two fingers that had been cut off in a farming accident, spinning tales about his "old codger" neighbors or the sad state of affairs in the world.

I never saw my grandfather angry until one night when my brother and I decided to challenge his command that we go to bed.

"You two get along now," Grandpa George said as he puffed on his trademark pipe, the stem of which had been chewed down over years of nervous gnawing. "Time for bed."

"I don't really feel tired." I laughed while my brother, Vincent, was conducting his own sit-down strike at the dining room table.

"You boys better listen to your Grandpa," Uncle Ken said, and he furiously rocked back and forth in the rocker in the living room. It was a wonder any of the furniture survived the fury of my father's younger siblings.

"We don't have school tomorrow," I countered. "We want to stay up and play."

"Oh, I think you better get on up to bed," Grandma Gertrude said, peering at us around the corner. "Grandpa means business."

Both Vincent and I were laughing and playing at the base of the stairs when the voice of the man who always grinned and laughed when he spoke suddenly erupted so violently that the vibration made the rafters of the old farmhouse shake.

"I said get to bed now, and you don't want to know what will happen if I have to get up out of this chair."

Uncle Ken smirked as Vincent and I stared at each other, momentarily dumbfounded. The color drained out of my brother's face, and I scrambled to my feet then raced him up the stairs to safety.

Yet I trusted this man implicitly when he stood atop the roof of our bathroom addition to my parents' home and reached his hand out with a wide grin, inviting me to join him on the roof.

I climbed the ladder and grabbed his hand, then he hoisted me atop the roof with one firm pull. He made me feel like a big little man. He made me feel secure.

Grandma Gertrude's hair was forever white in my mind. It should have been. She gave birth 15 times, once delivering the fraternal twins, Geri and Jerry. That wasn't the half of her momentous job. She had to feed and clothe the mob and, yes, my grandparents had a very traditional relationship in those days, which strictly defined their roles.

My grandfather was the provider and protector. My grandmother's job was to keep the house orderly and place food on the table.

Nephew or "lil' brother?"

I did consider growing up as the younger Wilmes among so many older role models odd. But the part fit me like a glove, and I naturally gravitated toward my uncles and aunts, following them along on errands, chores and other outings.

As I grew into adulthood, I would learn about my grandfather's stoic handling of a crisis and my grandmother's dual side that I never saw. She spoke two octaves above everyone else in the room, probably because she needed to be heard over the din of her children's energy.

She had given up much of her social life for the sake of her growing brood, but I never sensed that she regretted the sacrifice.

One thing George and Gertrude knew how to do was to simply be grandparents to their grandchildren. I never detected any signs of their interference in the raising of the next generation, and my definition of what a grandparent was solidified in those years of living just over a mile from their house.

My illusions of my grandparents' personas would be shattered later in life as I came to realize that not everything in this life is either black or white. I would learn no one is perfect, one of life's cruelest lessons to learn, especially when we're not perfect ourselves.

The first seven years of my life, stability reigned as a blessing.

We had many good neighbors. Though I don't remember it, my parents often related how my cousin Elmer would toddle over to our place from his parents' home a short distance away. We would take him to church with us.

I had enough trouble welcoming my younger brother when I was three, let alone sharing the spotlight with Elmer, who was a year older than I. I didn't like to share.

I was no longer the apple of my mother's eye. I greeted my

brother's arrival into the world with more than an ounce of jealousy as I watched my mother cradle him in her arms at the hospital and proudly introduce him to me.

The visiting ward at St. Francis Hospital had the smell and all the trappings of a sanitized institution that frightened me as a youngster. Seeing my brother swaddled in the white blanket as my mother gently placed him in my small arms and lap made me gulp in amazement.

I didn't want to break him, but I wasn't sure I knew what his presence in my life meant either. My mother was happy, so I guessed I could be happy as well, and thus I acted the part.

While I grew older, I relished the role of being a "little brother" when I would walk with my uncles behind the big red barn south of my grandparents' house and stood there as they exchanged teenage banter and smoked cigarettes.

"Don't you tell," Uncle Phil said.

Of course not. We had a code out there, a code of honor, a code of loyalty.

My grandfather raised some dairy cows and they also had some horses. One particular white stallion gave me the ride of my life when Aunt Dee hoisted me up on the beast and he took off as though he were running the Kentucky Derby.

"Hang on," I heard my aunt holler after me. She didn't have to worry about me following the command. My breath was heavy and strength greater than I had ever known as I held tightly to the horses' mane and somehow managed to get the animal to stop without my falling off.

I was also often invited to jump into the "Blue Goose," which was the first vehicle many of the younger aunts and uncles drove in preparation for getting their driver's licenses.

"Hang on, Marvin," Aunt Geri said, driving the vehicle rather recklessly while she tried to shift gears.

"You sure you know what you're doing?" Aunt Dee said as Geri ground the gears while stubbornly keeping at it until the Blue Goose finally groaned in relief, and Geri haltingly guided the car between the farm gateway's fence posts.

"Not really. I just know I've got to get the hang of this."

Getting the hang of it was the least of Geri's worries. All my aunts experienced Catholic boarding school in high school. It was part of Grandpa George's mantra as he sent his sons out to the field and his daughters off to high school after eighth grade. My father, too, attended school until the eighth grade, and then he was turned loose in the field.

George's sister Genevieve Wilmes was a nun. George believed that he would also have a priest in his family tree.

I absorbed his dream somewhere along the way in that first seven years, but God would have other ideas.

My uncle's shadow

My father's siblings were my greatest role models when I was young. They even encouraged my first love. Although her name escapes me today, I do remember sitting next to her on the bus was a special treat.

I implicitly trusted my elder relatives. They provided me with a blanket of security that was deeply felt, and from this foundation, I suppose, I developed a deep sense of family loyalty and love.

I demonstrated my trust one summer day while I sat on the lowboy as my uncles assisted my father in putting up a fresh cutting of hay bales. Ken drove the tractor and Phil stood tall as Tom and my father hoisted the bales onto the lowboy. I was seated safely near the wheel hub in the center of the lowboy wagon, but I recall wanting to be a big man like Phil.

I confidently got to my feet and began moving toward my uncle when suddenly the wagon lurched upward and back down again as Uncle Ken drove the tractor across the ditch. I was launched forward, flying through the air, and my mouth smashed against the side of the lowboy wagon. Uncle Phil grabbed thin air, just missing catching me and saving me from injury.

As I slowly regained a sense of reality, I felt warmth emerge from my mouth and I spit out the tooth that had become dislodged. While I grimaced at the sight of my own blood, I heard my father yelling at his youngest brother in a fit of rage.

"Are you all right?" my uncle Phil asked, and he rushed to my side.

I couldn't find the words to answer him. The pain of the dislodged tooth was secondary to my guilt at having Uncle Ken suffer my father's wrath.

It was my fault.

I thought I said the words aloud, but I actually hadn't. I was trying to stand up and be the little big man.

"What's wrong with you?" my father scolded. "Who taught you to drive?

Uncle Ken was silent while my father unleashed his anger, and I got off the wagon and started walking to the house, tooth in hand, leaving a blood trail behind.

"Are you all right?" My father's voice softened when he turned his attention to me.

I nodded, pointing to the blood and holding up my tooth for him to see. I silently nursed my wounds, and I headed back to the house, suffering more from the shock of the event than from any physical pain.

Two households were located on the George Wilmes' spread of land. The pasture in which this incident occurred would later become the central hub of my grandparents' world as they would build a house here in the early 70s.

They would build a huge monolithic structure that provided more than enough room after they began their empty-nest years. George would escape to the land he'd labored so hard over for many years, seeking solace and solitude, as Gertrude would create her own memories, constructing a sunroom filled with greenery and attempting to emerge from a life robbed of social contact due to the demands of raising such a large family.

In the basement, they had a pool table available as a tool to allow for many grandkids to connect with their grandfather in a competitive game that required more skill than luck.

I walked away from the scene of my lost tooth without expressing any sense of what I was thinking at the time of the accident. The fact remained, trying to stand up and join my uncle Phil was worth the effort. I'd made a move toward growing up, and in the process, I'd also lost a tooth.

We all lose something when we move toward something else. Sometimes we need a lifetime to learn that truth. We have to let go of some things in order to embrace others.

2 - TIPPIE

I let go of a lot of things in 1963, including the house that I grew up in.

My father had farmed with his father for nine years, and his brother Raymond was getting married in February of that year. My father was feeling the pressure to move out and to move on with his life.

I remember the day my father agonized over a decision he knew he had to make.

He stood before me, his head lowered, and somehow he looked older and rather tired. He lifted his cap and swiped his hand over his hair, which was always trimmed in a crew cut, and he shared his decision with my mother.

I was captivated by the strength and resolve he displayed, and I must have sensed that what he was about to say was going to affect my life forever.

"It's time to move on," he said. "I've had a good nine years, but it's time to do this on my own."

He was participating in a ritual of declaring freedom from his father. Reflecting on it later, I knew I heard grief in my father's voice. And I don't remember my mother saying one word.

Sometimes, though, she didn't have to. My parents shared a silent communication that often surpassed normal understanding. My view of love was largely shaped by my witnessing it between them every day.

My father, Alfred, wasted no time looking for a farm to buy, and never looked back. I was apprehensive, however. I didn't want to leave the security of my extended family's backyard.

I stared at our house for a long time as I hugged our mixed-breed collie, Tippie. The tire swing that hung from the tree next to the house would no longer provide comfort. I would be saying goodbye to my home. It was the first time in my young life I had grappled with loss.

Winds of change

I awoke on a cold and snowy January morning in my grandparents' house, knowing this was the last day of school for me here as we were moving that day.

Uncle Ken roused me out of bed, but the warmth underneath the covers was too precious to give up.

"Get away. I'm not going to school today," I said.

"Yes you are," Ken insisted as he pulled me out of my comfortable slumber and directed me downstairs to talk to my grandmother about the issue at hand.

"You will go to school," Grandma Gertrude said in no uncertain terms. "There will be no playing hooky."

"But Mama and Daddy are moving today."

"Yes, they are, and you'll join them after school," Ken said.

Traitor, I thought, *you just don't understand. I don't want to say goodbye.*

I was moving to a farm nearly 25 miles away, which was six miles west of Parnell, Missouri, population 250.

My second grade class would be comprised of 20 students. Life would be awkward, but joyful. I always viewed my experience growing up on a farm as a treasured part of my past, even though, like Grandpa Roy, farming wasn't in my blood.

Tippie and I would miss the old home place, but a new adventure beckoned.

When my parents picked me up at my grandparents' house after school that day, I ran to my mother and wrapped my arms around her.

I would have to let go of what I knew and embrace the unknown.

When I said goodbye to my grandparents and Uncle Ken and Aunt Dee, I left a piece of myself behind.

After we drove up to the two-story farmhouse and Vincent and I rushed out and frolicked in the snow with Tippie, I felt a familiar feeling settle in.

I was home again.

So I left the shadow of my uncle and aunts and moved to a farm several miles away. I had to let go of those heroes in my life and learn to stand on my own two feet, not always an easy task.

I had survived the nuns of St. Gregory's Catholic School, the ones with eyes in the back of their heads, and who could see around their black, flowing veils.

I joined the newly integrated second grade class of Northeast Nodaway RV. In the fall of 1962, the school districts of Parnell and Ravenwood merged.

I was taller than one of my classmates, Tom Birkenholz, and the lanky Ravenwood kid wasn't taking it lying down. I felt the competition and the heat.

Also, in this new school, I wanted to prove myself to my classmates.

Our second grade teacher, Mrs. B. K. Lewis, had horn-rimmed glasses behind which steely eyes stared right through you. Her deeply set dark eyes delivered an evil glare.

I one-upped her one day after she'd left the room to run an errand as I took command of the situation and began mimicking her as though I were teaching the class. I would later learn much to my consternation that the woman whose rough exterior I modeled was one of my maternal grandmother's friends.

That didn't protect me though from her wrath while I was performing for my classmates; a thunderous clap from the hand that collided with my backside echoed against the backdrop of my howl.

The classroom erupted in laughter, and Tom Birkenholz likely took the greatest pleasure in my humiliation when I was brought directly to the principal's office.

The flights and fancies of a second grader in a small school, coming from the rigid confines of a Catholic school, gave me more confidence, I suppose, to challenge the borders of common sense.

I immediately befriended David Miller and Larry Wray, and

we became known for a short time as the Three Musketeers. We all three had a delightful time finding mischief, including the teasing of the milk delivery man.

He was a heavyset twenty-something chap who had a jovial sense of humor and enjoyed our banter just as much as we enjoyed dishing it out to him. We nicknamed him "Grandma," a name he disdained. After all, he was just trying to make a living, and he had to deal with these three bratty second graders.

Our small school provided ample fodder for the development of legends.

A kindly, frail looking woman lived down the lane, and during one afternoon recess, she came out of her house onto the road that led to our elementary school.

In her arms she held a black cat and stood directly in our path. In my second grade imagination, I easily mistook her friendly overtures toward my friends and me for something more sinister.

"Would you like to come in for some cookies and milk?" she asked as she gently petted her feline companion.

Our response was motivated from fear of the unknown. I imagined that Parnell had its very own wicked witch and though we didn't have a bed to crawl under, my classmates and I turned and ran back to the schoolyard.

One classmate, Bob Welch, was her neighbor. He knew she was a lonely old widow who probably wondered why these young kids had to be so mean to someone as frail as she was. He made the legend of the imagined witch stand out in my memory even more as he related how she had this black cauldron in her house and stirred up delicious soup to boil little boys in.

Later, I would learn from my mother and grandmother that she was as harmless as the kitten she'd held in her arms.

In this new school, I experienced a freedom I hadn't felt before. I had stepped out of the shadows of my uncles and aunts and the awesome traditions of my father's family. Here, I was frightened and a boy of courage all at once.

The small parish of St. Joseph's Catholic Church in Parnell was more serene than the huge monolithic St. Gregory's Catholic Church in Maryville. My parents attended church every Sunday, including Holy Days of Obligation and this was never to be questioned by us.

My religious upbringing would initially be influenced by Father Andrew, an elderly priest with thick, bifocal glasses that still couldn't help him see. I never saw him smile and I felt no kindness in his lack of patience.

I would be exposed to the saintly teachings of my grandmother's half aunt, Lena Logan. She didn't wear dentures. Her tongue would thrust in and out as she excitedly shared the tale of how she took over the wheel of her husband's car when he'd suffered a fatal heart attack. She didn't know how to drive, but she saved herself that day.

The way she saw it, Jesus had saved her. All you had to do to assure your soul was saved if something tragic happened was holler out to Jesus, "Jesus save me," and according to Lena, he would do it.

He did it for her; he would do it for us.

Reality versus illusion

I wearily rubbed the sleep from my eyes and gingerly placed my bare feet on the hardwood floor in my boyhood home. My younger brother snored lightly in his bed in the corner of our room.

As I followed the voices in the breezeway of our house, I stopped in my tracks, seeing the freshly skinned animal carcasses hanging from the ceiling and my father and uncles busy cutting and cleaning the fresh meat.

"What are you doing up?" my father asked, taken aback that I had come upon their work.

"I couldn't sleep," I said while I tried to take in the scene before me.

"We're just butchering up some hogs. Now go back to bed."

My Uncle Phil glanced at me and gave me a wink. He flashed me a grin.

I didn't know why my father told me that little white lie. Only many years later while Uncle Phil and Aunt Karen were dining in our Parnell home would he recall bagging three deer and butchering them in the middle of the night.

When I realized the story Phil was sharing with my father at the dinner table concerned the same night I crashed my father's "hog" butchering, I challenged the elders about this.

Phil flashed me a smile again with a wink and I realized the last laugh was on me for believing the fabrication for all those years.

Reality had played a trick on my mind. What I remembered about the event was in no way what happened. I accepted my elders' explanation because I had no reason to question it.

Consequently, the memory remained undisturbed for many years before an external event, a conversation between my father and uncle recalling their version, forced me to confront the memory and reconstruct it.

Then I validated their account and determined the issues brought up by the truth impacted what I'd previously believed. Thus, the lie had created an illusion, and in the process of interpretation, it revealed a flaw in my logical assumptions.

I hadn't totally trusted the assumption I was left with at the time and had tucked the "hog butchering" memory away. I didn't need long to retrieve the memory as fresh facts were presented and I was able to understand the event from a new perspective.

Thus, "the process," an interpretation by which a person views the world around him and that forms a person's coping mechanism is set into motion.

In my life, I went through many watersheds, challenges and experiences from which to refine my philosophy on life, but I had no idea during the year of 1963 that this single year would define so many beliefs for me in the future.

As a seven-year-old, much of how I dealt with loss and change was already established. As a carefree youngster, I had no interest in processing the events of the year from a spiritual, much less psychological, view. That would come in time.

One such memory from 1963 involved the family dog, my best friend, Tippie.

I used to love watching the television show, Lassie. Not just any Lassie—the one with the boy they called Timmy, and of course, he was my age.

As illusions are birthed in the questions we don't ask, the things we accept at face value or in our desire to not really care to learn the truth by further explanations, I began a journey with man's best friend that would also surprise me with facts hidden from view.

Did I know the truth all along, or did I always believe Tippie, the mixed breed collie, was my dog?

Peggy's dog

*"I accepted a teaching position at Southeast in Kansas City,"
my grandmother suddenly announced to Peggy.*

*"Oh, Mom," she said. "That's wonderful, but what about the
farm?"*

"We've decided to sell the farm," Roy interjected.

*Peggy looked at her father and realized he had a tear in his
eye. He'd worked so hard through his life to own something he
could call his own, and now he was having to let it go.*

"We'd like you to keep Tippie for us."

*Peggy's heart skipped a beat. Keep him, but her father and he
had been such faithful companions for so many years.*

*"Oh Dad," she said as she reached up to hug him. "We'll take
good care of him. Marvin and Vincent will have lots of fun with
him, I'm sure. Thank you."*

Holding on and letting go.

For each of us, life's experiences are as individual as the
snowflakes in a winter storm.

Tippie moved with us when we settled into our new
farmhouse. I remember very little about the move except that the
two-story house seemed three times the size of our previous single-
floor home on the farm.

"Where's Tippie?" my father asked my mother one chilly
morning after we'd been living at the farm for a week.

"I don't know. I haven't seen him all morning."

When I got home from school later that day, I realized Tippie
was missing. "I'll look for him," I volunteered as my mother
shared with me the news that he couldn't be found.

Nightfall arrived and still no Tippie.

My heart ached for the missing collie.

I had to accept his disappearance as a fact. No tears fell; only a
sadness filled my heart.

Often, reflecting in the quiet stillness of the Missouri night, I
imagined Tippie walking along the road searching for and trying to
make his way back to the Wilmes homestead.

"I'm sure he probably got lost as he headed home," Grandpa

Roy said to me when he learned of the disappearance the following Saturday. He looked toward the east with a solemn face as he made the declarative statement, even though Tippie's former home was west of us.

My grandparents often visited on the weekends and stayed in the guest bedroom upstairs. I could tell Grandpa Roy was deeply troubled by Tippie's disappearance. He bit his lower lip and looked to the horizon with a sadness. He was the last one to give up the search for Tippie.

I was touched when I saw my father's arms envelope my mother from behind while he offered his support for her loss.

Just a boy, I was so involved in my own sense of loss, I never made the connection to what Tippie meant to my mother and grandfather.

I would eventually learn that Tippie was "Grandpa's dog" when my father shattered another one of my illusions in adulthood.

Things made sense with the new information, and I later understood that my grandfather believed Tippie had tried to find my grandparents' homestead northeast of Parnell in the rolling hills of Worth County.

Decades later, I put the unsolved mystery of Tippie's disappearance to rest. I came to believe that shortly after we moved to the Parnell farm, Tippie went home to where all good dogs go when they die.

As I came to understand the jigsaw puzzle pieces of 1963 and put them back together on the canvass of my life, I began to understand myself even better.

Trixie

My yearning for Tippie soon faded after my mother, who had also suffered a loss because Tippie was her childhood companion, decided it was time for the family to move on in its grief.

Shortly after Tippie disappeared, my mother took my brother, Vincent, and me to a quaint two-story house on the east side of Maryville to look at a puppy.

When we entered the woman's living room, we noticed there, in plentiful supply, dozens of sock monkeys she had created for sale to the public.

The middle-aged woman presented us with the cutest black

and white terrier you would ever see, who playfully jumped up on the sides of the basket she was using as a bed. My brother and I immediately dropped to our knees to pet the feisty puppy and instantly fell in love with her.

We named her Trixie.

Trixie took to my brother and me with the boundless energy that Tippie, in his old age, could never achieve.

The wide expanse of the farm provided a fantastic playground for my brother and me. Trixie followed us everywhere, keeping up with my father, too, as he tended the farm while we were at school.

I embraced the adventures that moving away from my extended family afforded me, which was worlds away from my previous childhood.

For every child, a day arrives when innocence is lost.

For me, that bend in the road was directly ahead.

3 – TRAGEDY AND SECRETS

On a sunny Sunday afternoon in June of 1963, my maternal grandparents had come from Parkville and spent the weekend as they often did. They were standing in the kitchen bidding us farewell, something Grandma Tuttle always had trouble finishing up.

The Norman Rockwell portrait in my mind of Mom, Dad, my grandparents, Vincent and me gathered around the kitchen table is frozen forever in my mind.

The phone rang.

Mom answered the phone, "Hello."

She put her hand to her cheek, and her countenance changed instantly. It appeared this was not a good call.

A cloud of anticipation hung in the kitchen as we all waited to find out why my mother seemed so concerned. Her voice trembled, her face turned white and her expression became even more grave.

"Oh no," she wailed. Her head fell into her hand, and she nearly dropped the phone.

I stood there, speechless, wondering what had caused this change in her. Fearing something horrible, I still wasn't prepared for what came next.

"Elmer's gone."

At first, I couldn't grasp what she had said.

"Oh dear." Grandma Naomi stood there, unable to provide any comfort as she put her hand to her mouth and tears began to form. My grandfather sat down in a chair, shaking his head in disbelief. My father seemed simply frozen in fear.

"Stevie, Elmer and Alan were playing down by the river. I'm not sure what happened, but Elmer drowned."

I didn't wait to see what happened next. I could not absorb this news. I couldn't believe it. I wanted to scream, but I had no voice.

Elmer

Tag, you're it." Elmer just barely touched my shoulder as I attempted to escape his far-reaching grasp.

He was feeling victorious, and he jumped up and down and let out a war hoop. I turned to try to tag my other cousins, Alan, Steve and Norman or my brother, Vincent, but they were more agile than I as we all played in the empty, monolithic, wire grain bin on Uncle Bernard's farm.

Steve was the oldest son of Bernard and Cecelia Wilmes, and Elmer came next. Alan and I were the same age.

Bernard was the oldest of George and Gertrude's family, and he and his wife, Cecelia, were my godparents.

My brother and I often pestered Mom and Dad to go on a Sunday outing to Bernard and Cecelia's, and this particular memory had a strange but lasting effect on me.

It was and has always been my only memory of Elmer alive.

Try as I might, only one other recollection remains: the lifeless body of Elmer in his casket.

My cousins Alan and Steve began carrying their cross the day Elmer drowned, especially Steve, who couldn't act to save his brother. Neither Elmer nor Steve could swim. I often imagined my oldest cousin standing on the river bank while his brother Alan ran to get help.

"It's a good thing Steve didn't try to save Elmer," my father declared. "They would have lost two sons."

I sat on the cistern near the front porch of our rural Parnell home and cried.

"No God, not Elmer. It can't be true."

There was no consoling me, and no one came to my side, since my parents wisely let me experience the tidal wave of grief that assaulted me.

Despite my disbelief, death had come to park its carcass on my doorstep.

Scars and fears

The newspaper headline the next day spoke of my cousin's death as rescue crews searched the murky bottom of the river for his body.

When the body was found, all hope was taken from his mother, Aunt Cecelia, who was led along like a rag doll in her grief. I watched her walk into the house consoled by my Uncle Bernard. The image would be permanently etched in my mind. They were my godparents. Things like this just weren't supposed to happen.

We were at my uncle's home for hours in wake of the tragedy. Vince had gone with our Uncle Ken and Norman to assist with some chores. Word came that Vincent had been hurt and was rushed to the doctor.

My mother totally broke down this time, unable to hold her worst fears at bay. Had the river taken another life?

No, the family comforted her, he'd fallen off the wagon and had a gash to his head that needed stitches. This was something our family became used to as Vincent, the more adventurous and the more accident prone of the two of us, often needed emergency care.

Months later, Vincent, my mother and I were riding on a tall load of hay as my father maneuvered the wagon through the tree-lined road that overshadowed the west boundary of our farm.

Vincent was sitting in between my mother and me one minute, and the next he was gone, a branch having knocked him from his perch.

"Vincent!" my mother gasped, and she grabbed the air where he had once been.

In an instant, a scene flashed through my mind that the wheels of the wagon might have run over my brother.

"Stop," my mother yelled from her seat, and I joined her in an effort to get my father to stop the tractor. Scenes of my lost tooth briefly played through my mind, but this was much more serious.

I peered over the hay bales and was relieved to see my brother lying on his back, spread eagled, crying, but all right, far away from the wheels of the wagon.

"One minute you were there and the next, bam. I didn't even see it coming," I said to my little brother who climbed back atop the wagon.

My father went into a frenzy, and my mother just ignored it.

"Let's go home," she said. "Are you hurt?" she asked Vincent.

"He's mainly scared, I'll bet," I chimed in.

"Yeah, I don't really know what hit me."

My brother was tough all right. A real champ.

As we got back to the house, my father parked the lowboy of hay and shut off the tractor. My mother, Vincent and I scrambled to solid ground.

Before we even landed, my mother fell into my father's arms and wept, and he comforted her as I had seen him do many times. The beauty of my parents' love never left me as I saw them angry at each other one minute and making up the next. My father was never afraid to show his affection for my mother.

The seriousness of what had just happened began to sink in when my mother released her emotions. I looked at my brother and realized what had just happened wasn't funny.

He could have been seriously hurt, or worse.

The next year, Dad got to work and cleared the roadway of the trees and built a new fence line. I'm not sure if Vincent's accident had anything to do with it, but the farm looked much better afterward.

Swimming trauma

"This is where it happened," my Uncle Raymond said, pointing out to his brothers and me where Elmer's drowning had occurred. We stood on the rugged terrain of the Nodaway River.

I surveyed the underbrush and the jagged river bank and felt a chill run up my spine in witnessing the river waters below.

I was fascinated while my uncles were busy speculating about how the accident might have occurred.

Deep in thought, I felt someone grasp me around the waist, lift me up and fling me through the air, while holding me firmly in his grasp. But in that moment I didn't feel the assurance that the hands wouldn't let me go.

My heart leapt into my throat and I heard laughter. I then realized the hands were my father's.

I tried to scream, but it stuck in my throat.

I laughed along with everyone else at the event, shaking off the fear since I was still processing this experience, and the memory buried itself deep into my consciousness as I couldn't deal with it at that exact moment.

My cousins were just being boys; they were simply playing. How could Elmer be here one minute and gone the next?

The riverbank memory stayed behind that day, and I left it where it had lodged itself. Deep in my subconscious. I know today that my father was, in fact, dealing with his own jumbled emotions—he sometimes wasn't as direct as my mother.

The Wilmes boys were raised to be stoic, to not show emotion, to be tough. My father wanted to pass that onto me, but I had more of my mother's traits in me than his. Vincent was the one who was more like him.

I would challenge lots of my father's visions of who I should be in my life, and I would struggle to find my way through his traditions and expectations.

While the blur of those difficult days passed, I turned eight that summer. However, as I accompanied my parents to Price Funeral Home in Maryville, I walked up to Elmer's casket, knelt beside it and looked at his lifeless body.

This was the first of many family rosaries that I would attend in our Catholic faith.

I'm not sure what I believed about Elmer's death at that juncture in my life. I felt an emptiness when I knelt beside him and offered up a weak prayer. I spent a few seconds with him, taking in the reality that he was gone.

I don't think I really prayed at all. I just stared at him, wondering how life could be so cruel.

I walked toward Bernard and Cecelia and all my cousins and followed my parents lead in shaking their hands. I just shook their hands numbly, still not able to believe what had happened.

I'm sure I went to the funeral, yet I don't remember any of it. That first night, I took the memory of Elmer lying lifeless in the casket and the riverbank prank played by my father and buried them deep.

His joke was all in fun, all in jest, and I'm sure the sliver of film that runs in my mind is simply too traumatic to view many loops of. For the majority of my life I would attribute my failing to learn to swim as being passed on from my mother's phobia of the same.

It had never occurred to me that in my own way, I had been traumatized by Elmer's death. I would love water, learn to water ski and even trek on a tiny paddle boat far from the Waikiki shore on the island of Oahu as a Marine. On that trip, I would learn that my paddle mate couldn't swim, either, as the waves smashed into our small vessel tipping it to 45-degree angles.

Never had I engaged in such agile paddling to get back to safety. Fear has no fury like staring at the ocean, knowing you would likely sink rather than swim.

The forbidden topic

"I'm gonna miss Elmer," I said to my cousin Alan as we eavesdropped on the adult conversations taking place in my uncle's house.

"Yeah, I still can't believe he's gone. Sometimes it's like a bad dream. I keep thinking he'll come downstairs and life will be the way it was."

"How's Stevie doing?"

"Not very good." Alan stared straight ahead while he relived the events of the tragic day again. "He couldn't swim you know."

"I know." I didn't offer anything else. I had nothing more to say.

We shared stories about Elmer, and our boyish laughs drifted into the living room. My mother spied us outside the window, conversing.

We still were trying to make sense of what had happened.

I glanced through the window and saw urgency in my mother's eyes as she silently excused herself from the murmurs of my extended family's small talk. I knew that look well. I wasn't sure why, but I sensed Alan and I were in trouble.

"You boys need to go play, go on. We don't have to talk about Elmer right now." Then to make it perfectly clear to us why she was issuing this mandate, she glanced inside at Aunt Cecelia, then back at us. "Go on now."

Neither one of us wanted to cause any more pain, so we ran away from the house and started playing again.

I didn't realize it at the time, but I would literally live out my mother's reprimand many years into the future. I never really talked about Elmer from that day forward.

No one else did either.

It wasn't that Elmer's memory was extinguished by a deliberate act of omission, it was just easier for me not to ask questions about Elmer, and likewise, no one saw the need to talk about him with me.

Visiting my grandmother's new house in the 1970s as a young man, my eyes would often drift to the black and white photograph of Elmer surrounded by exotic flowers and other knick knacks she decorated her living room with.

Never once did I say, "Grandma, that's a nice picture of Elmer. Can you tell me about him?"

Instead, I would ponder how she could possibly display that picture so boldly.

The photograph was comforting, but at the same time animated a sense of fear inside of me. Seeing it reminded me that he'd died. I never realized that I could just walk up to the picture, pick it up and quip about what great fun we'd had playing in a grain bin once upon a time, years before.

Grandma Wilmes never knew how that picture revived Elmer's spirit and kept his memory alive for me. Something inside stirred every time I sat in that living room and viewed the picture.

Without tallying the cost, I packed the trauma away and continued on. Loss was something that you didn't talk about. You were expected to move on.

And I became very good at it.

Circle of life

The fall brought the harvest, and my father installed the orange corn picker on the front of his Allis Chalmers D-17 tractor then headed off to the field pulling the wooden wagon behind him.

While I watched him go, I smiled as Trixie barked and playfully followed my father into the field. I returned to my duties of cleaning out the hog shed.

When my father returned from the field for supper, he had a somber face.

"I'm sorry," he confessed, and he sat in the kitchen chair like a defeated man. I knew what he had to say next was probably not good.

"Everything was going along fine, I worried about Trixie barking and playing around the corn picker, I even hollered at her and told her to get away, and for a while it looked as though she had listened."

I held my breath. I knew what was next.

"Then there was this yelp and….."

I didn't need to hang around to hear the end of the sentence. Trixie was gone.

This was to begin a long line of canine losses in my life.

With that, I unconsciously came down with a dog phobia. I resolved to keep my distance from that point on. Even though I still liked dogs, I didn't have to love them.

If I did, something bad was sure to happen.

Loss of innocence

I couldn't have told you who the president of the United States was on the morning of November 21st, 1963, but I remember that snapshot of a day as if it were yesterday.

I was coming out of the boys' bathroom at the Parnell Elementary School when Bob Welch delivered the news.

"President Kennedy has been shot."

That evening, my family and I were gathered around the black and white images that moved across the screen. This year of loss was topped off by John F. Kennedy's assassination.

His assassin's name had become a household word…Lee Harvey Oswald.

A single gunshot had felled our nation's leader. A river had drowned my cousin. A corn picker had killed Trixie.

There was no hiding from tragedy. It was everywhere.

The following Sunday as I lay on the floor sprawled out in front of the black and white set, something incredible occurred. In what seemed like slow motion, a man erupted from the crowd and something akin to fireworks could be heard. Then I witnessed Lee Harvey Oswald, the alleged assassin of President Kennedy, sort of fold and collapse on live television.

My father was up and out of his chair. And in the same moment, I too was on my feet as we both expressed our awe and amazement that Lee Harvey Oswald, President Kennedy's presumed murderer, had himself been felled by an assassin's bullet.

The nation's trauma became part of my own personal traumas. Somehow I merged it in with just enough denial to move forward into 1964 with little fanfare.

I had lost something else in 1963.

No longer did I feel the secure embrace of my grandfather's strong hands as I climbed up on top of the "roof" of life.

4 – CHILDHOOD FAITH

"Kyrie eleison."

"Kyrie eleison."

I studied hard to follow the phonograph record's directions in pronouncing the Latin words I needed to master to be an altar server at our small Catholic parish in Parnell.

I met the challenge with enthusiasm. Fortunately, the church was going through a massive change and overhaul with what was called the Second Vatican Council, and the Latin form of the mass had been replaced with a more user-friendly English version.

Well, seen as fortunate by me. My father's generation embraced the changes going on in the church less than enthusiastically.

As an altar server, I would walk beside the priest down the row of parishioners who knelt at the communion railing.

Change didn't stop with the elimination of the Latin. Eventually, communion railings became obsolete. Rules regarding the handling of the host changed. What once was sacred and could never be touched by anyone except a priest was now put into the chalice at the back of the church by those parishioners who chose to go to communion.

Nuns, who once were shrouded in the black robes of their habits, threw off the traditional garb for a more current look. They were no longer recognizable by what they wore.

This revolution in the church was felt in our home as my mother and father were very active in trying to understand and to attempt to slow down the changes.

However, change was roaring through every social fiber of the nation, and with the Vietnam War hovering over my childhood and racial unrest and riots across the nation, my existence in rural northwest Missouri was rather tame by comparison.

The more radical changes in culture were slow in arriving, but when they did, it was no easier for us to cope with them.

I was fascinated with the religious life. I believed in God. I never questioned my parents' guidance in this area of my life—until one day while we were driving home from Mass at the Parnell parish I asked about an issue that challenged my father. From his response, I knew he had been waiting for it. He wasn't happy the day had arrived.

"Are Catholics the only ones who go to heaven? I mean, what about other Christian faiths? Don't they believe in the same thing?"

My father and mother exchanged glances.

"No one says that people of other faiths don't go to heaven," my mother responded.

"It's just that Jesus founded the Catholic faith," Alfred said. "He told Peter, 'Upon this rock I will build my church.' Peter was the first pope. Other denominations came later, and they established their own churches."

"I see," I said.

My father glanced back at me as I took his answer under consideration.

I didn't say anything. Yet, I wondered. Where in the Bible was the word Catholic used?

I was one of a new generation that was destined to question the fabric of American society.

My brother, Vincent, was beside me in the back seat, deep in thought about something else. Unlike me, he didn't really get involved in all these debates with my father. We were different that way.

I didn't realize that life as I knew it as an older brother was about to change in an even more dramatic way when I reached preadolescence.

Surprise announcement

Things were a blur the day I came home from school and my mother had my brother and me sit down for a special announcement.

She was absolutely beaming while she prepared us for her news.

"You know, boys, for a long time it has been just the four of us. But what would you think if I told you we're going to have a new arrival in our family?"

She paused to allow us both to weigh the gravity of her words.

"I'm going to have a baby."

"Really." Vincent grinned and giggled, and his dimples popped to life.

I was initially at a loss for words. I attempted to wrap my mind around this concept; after all, it had been my brother and me for so long.

"Your new baby brother or baby sister should arrive around February," our mother said as she continued to bask in her happiness. "I guess we'll have lots of changes around here."

"Yeah, for certain," I agreed. "Wow, that's exciting."

I wasn't sure I was that convincing. I do know after my mother delivered this news, Vincent and I didn't compare notes about how we felt.

I walked out of the two-story farmhouse, took to the gravel road in front of our house and walked down the hill toward the bannister-less bridge at the bottom of the hill.

I had just been punched in the stomach with the proclamation. I was 11 years old, a sixth grader, in my last year at the Parnell Elementary School, and I wasn't quite sure how I should react to this news.

I was surprised at the fears that assaulted my sensibilities. Somewhere deep in my psyche, this announcement triggered a sense of loss, much like when we'd first moved here to Parnell.

While I threw rocks into the creek below, I pondered what this meant in my life. Being a big brother to a newborn baby was the last thing I had on my list of things to do as I prepared to enter into my teen years.

Labor pains

The winter rain was turning the blacktop road to Maryville into a smooth, velvety surface during the drive with our family of four and my Uncle Joe and Aunt Donna—my father at the wheel. We were headed to a unique family tradition of a mountain oyster fry at Uncle Raymond and Aunt Bert's.

Annually, my father would sell about 60 head of Angus cattle that he had fed for the past year at the St. Joseph stockyards, and he would purchase another 60 head to feed for the upcoming year.

Raymond and Joe would help him each year, including when the veterinarian would come and send the cattle through their vaccinations, tagging and castrations.

The annual "mountain oyster" feast was the reward for a job well done, and one delicacy my Grandma Tuttle never cared for, though one time she wasn't told about the delicacy placed before her and she thought it was absolutely delicious.

The feast also provided my elders with a social event that always ended in late night pitch or pinochle. I, too, quickly learned the art of these card games so I could join in the festivities.

I was seated in the back seat between Joe and Donna when I saw the large farm truck that had crossed the center line move toward us in what seemed like slow motion.

No driver was visible behind the wheel as my father slammed on his brakes and our car skidded across the rain-soaked pavement. The car was slowing, but it wouldn't stop.

My brother was sitting in the middle between my father and mother, and I instantly thought of her condition when I realized we weren't going to be able to avoid the head-on collision.

Dad had brought the family sedan to almost a complete stop as the driver of the vehicle suddenly appeared and tried to steer out of the way. But his efforts were too late.

The huge truck smacked the front end of our car, causing both vehicles to come to an abrupt halt.

My mother's hands were shaking, and my father asked if she was all right. I saw fear in her eyes, and I instantly knew why. She was worried about the baby.

My father got out of the car and immediately confronted the driver, who had been trying to retrieve something from the floor of

35

the cab. He apologized profusely and pleaded for my father not to report the accident.

My father refused and we all waited patiently for the Highway Patrol to respond after my father called them from a rural farmhouse.

After a time, it was obvious my mother and her baby were okay.

When all was said and done, we learned that the driver was an ex-con, which explained the reason for his reluctance to report the accident. Fortunately, though, no one was seriously hurt as a result of the collision.

I wasn't used to my mother's pregnancy and secretly wished it would be over soon. This baby stuff wasn't all it was cracked up to be.

Mashed potatoes and gravy

The day of David Michael Wilmes' birth, my brother and I were at school.

I had envisioned that the birth would occur with my mother scurrying around and shaking my father out of his slumber and screaming that he needed to take her to the hospital.

This was not an *I Love Lucy* show, though: This was real life, and the anticipation of bringing David home was changing everything in my environment.

He weighed six pounds, six ounces and had blue eyes. And the date of his birth was February 7th, 1967, she went calmly to the hospital while we were at school.

My parents were already considering how to expand the physical capacity of our house to allow for this unexpected addition to the family. After all, weren't they starting over? Vincent would be nine soon.

"Both Vincent and I have brown eyes and David has blue eyes," I said, presenting an argument to my mother that seemed perfectly logical to me. "That means there probably won't be any more kids."

"Maybe." My mother just smiled at me.

I was amazed at the small size of the baby boy she brought home. My dad boasted that he could hold David in the palm of his hand, and he did so.

I couldn't wait to feed my little brother, so I quickly rounded up a plate of mashed potatoes and gravy.

My mother looked at me and just laughed.

"What?" I asked, puzzled.

"You've got a lot to learn about raising a baby, Marvin. He can't eat mashed potatoes just yet."

My mother quietly fed David without further explanation. She had a way of explaining things, sometimes without words and sometimes with just enough information so you didn't want to ask for any more.

My parents had a skip in their steps while they busied themselves with the task of remodeling the basement as a family room for Vincent, David and me, moving their bedroom downstairs by transforming the extra room off the living room and building on an addition that added a utility room, a walk-in porch and a bathroom.

They hired a local carpenter from the church, Robert Spire, and I tagged along on some of the shopping trips with my parents for carpet, ceiling tiles and furniture.

My father helped eight-month-old David put his mark on the old pump in the backyard by carving his name and "1967" into the cement.

David became very active in that first year, though my mother dismissed Vincent's and my enthusiasm at getting David to walk.

Vincent and I put him up against the wall numerous times and encouraged him to walk toward us.

To my mother and father's amazement, we had David walking at the age of eight months, and it was a feat of accomplishment that Vincent and I deservedly shared with our younger brother.

To say we spoiled our brother was an understatement. At the age of 12, I learned the art of changing diapers, feeding him baby food and watching him grow into a happy toddler.

As for David being the last one in our family, if I didn't want our family to grow that idea would be a lost hope.

On a blustery March day in 1968, I spied my mother returning from town carrying a bag of groceries.

When she came into the house, she smiled at me.

"You boys might want to help me carry the groceries in. I'm pregnant again."

My mother delivered the news with such grace and simplicity, I had no idea this newfound fertility was the answer to many years of prayer.

As for me, I was getting used to the idea of welcoming another brother or sister.

The stolen goodbye

The year of my brother Dean's birth was far from calm on the world stage, let alone in northwest Missouri.

That year, Martin Luther King Jr. and Robert Kennedy would both be felled by assassins' bullets, but the 13-year-old who pondered these tragedies while walking aimlessly through rolling green pastures of our farm was grappling with deeper issues about the meaning of life and death.

In April of 1968, my uncle Jerry took his bride, Odelia Moffett, who unwittingly stole my heart as one of my favorite aunts.

At 20, she wore her brunette hair in a high-spun beehive and radiated innocence. She was graceful, modest and sweet all at the same time. Likely far from perfect, but as storybook weddings go, I was captured by their union.

The couple were the next inhabitants of my boyhood home, and our visiting the scene of my roots for supper one evening was more than enchanting for me. Odelia was the gracious hostess and showered Vincent and me with more than enough attention.

As I ended my junior high career approaching my eighth grade graduation, Louise Stephenson came to our house to announce her husband had lost his battle to cancer.

Steve Stephenson had been the country gentleman who had visited our house a time or two to partake of a good card game and friendly chit chat. He wore a top hat and smoked a pipe, and his personality was bigger than life as he shared with my father stories of faith and the Knights of Columbus both were a member of.

I never tired of his stories, and to hear of his death had me pondering going to his wake and experiencing the grief I now felt at the delivery of the news from his wife, Louise.

"Marvin and Vincent, it's my wishes you don't go to his services," Louise was saying as I snapped out of my trip down memory lane, remembering the jovial nature of a good family friend. "I want you to remember him the way he was."

I was stunned at the mandate, wanted to protest, but if I had any courage to say anything, my mother's words cut me off.

"Don't worry, Louise. They will always have fond memories of Steve. I think that's a good idea."

When Louise drove off, Vince and I went to play while my mother and father processed their own grief.

This time, the silence demanded of me seemed unfair. My heart ached because I really felt the need to say goodbye.

Water's revenge

The summer brought my 13th birthday and much work occupied my brother and me on the farm. I had been learning to drive the tractor, and my father trusted Vincent and me to put up the hay on our own.

We became more interested in earning money, and we went into business with Grandpa Roy. He provided the lawn mower, gas and pickup; we provided the boy power.

It was the first and last year we operated the business since it was profitable for Vincent and me, but hardly for Roy, who weighed the investment of gas, time and lawn mower repairs against $2 to $5 lawn mowing jobs as being not so profitable.

One day, we were walking some rows of beans in the July heat, looking for and destroying the dreaded cockle burr.

My father paused to take a drink of water, and we saw my mother approach in the family car. The look on her face appeared all too familiar.

This time my Uncle Phil had the cross to bear. As my mother recounted the story of how Phillip, Tom, Ken and their twin cousins, Mike and Pat, were haying and took a break to take a dip in the farm pond, I felt the breath whish out of my lungs.

Mike had somehow gotten in trouble while swimming and was thrashing wildly in the water. Phil was immediately by his side and tried to rescue his cousin. His efforts were thwarted by Mike's panic.

Phil went under as well, and struggle as he might, the panic displayed by Mike was too strong for him to overcome.

Donald Michael Wilmes died that day, July 12th, 1968, a victim of drowning.

In the aftermath, Grandpa George had to defend my uncle against the wrath of an angered father and his own brother, Hubert.

The anger was an element of a grief larger than life itself, but Phillip had taken the emotional barrage nonetheless.

Once again, I was protected from the seamier side of life, the realities of death, and things were quickly resolved, and we moved on.

But I knew Phillip had experienced a trauma that was a huge burden to bear, just like my cousin Steve.

When a fire broke out in Ravenwood and took the life of a classmate's father, the rumor mill in Ravenwood burned hot with gossip.

I hated gossip. I hated the thought of people not taking the full picture of what had occurred in a person's life to heart.

As I entered high school, my emotions were a mess. I was going through many changes I didn't even understand.

My grandparents lived two blocks from the high school, my Aunt Rita worked as a secretary in the school—and I came into contact with a bully. My reactions to everything going on in my life over the summer of 1968 and beyond amazed even my parents.

They had no idea what was going on with me. The truth of the matter was neither did I.

I increasingly became a defender of the underdog. Any criticism of my generation would get under my skin.

I didn't have enough knowledge about grief to know that Mike's death had triggered a deep wound in my psyche.

I was angry, but I didn't know at what.

Until January of 1969.

The good die young

My father's family gathered for a New Year's Eve card party at the Maryville Knights of Columbus Hall and I played as the partner of Aunt Odelia much of the night.

We finally won as partners and were delighted at our good fortune.

That would be the last time I would see Odelia alive.

She soon came down with a flu virus, which turned into pneumonia.

Death moved in quickly and without mercy. We had no

warning, no time to prepare.

I had prayed fervently for Odelia's healing, a last vestige of something I learned as a tutor of our faith. I naturally gravitated to belief in God, going so far as to conduct a Mass for my family one snowbound Sunday, complete with blanketed garb to represent the priestly attire.

Uncle Jerry asked me to be an altar boy at the funeral service. My job was to carry the crucifix. Standing there at the back of the church holding the ornament, I watched my uncle's grief consume him.

When I stared at the figure on the cross, I couldn't understand God or Christ at the moment.

Two days before, I had come into the house from doing my chores when I saw my mother fall into my father's arms after she completed the phone call she was on.

"She's gone."

I couldn't digest those words. This was the same kitchen where I'd heard unbelievable words six years before that Elmer was dead. I couldn't accept that Odelia had succumbed so quickly to illness after we'd laughed and played cards together on New Year's Eve.

Why?

The question hung in the air in my room as anger welled up in my soul. This time I couldn't return from the edge of grief.

"Why would You take someone so young?" I shook my fist at heaven.

Now, I stood staring at the figure on the cross I was holding, while I endured the emotional outbursts, the sobs and my own uncle's torture at that funeral as he was asking those same questions.

I felt the supports of my childhood faith crack, and after that day, I put away God as some far-off fairy tale, barely understanding anything about the faith I'd grown up with.

I went through the motions, and my parents never noticed because I still said the things I was expected to say or do. In time, after leaving home, I would fall away from church while still professing a belief in God.

The reason for this apostasy was a simple one. I had prayed for Aunt Odelia.

She had died anyway. God had turned a deaf ear.

Pneumonia was added to my list of life fears along with water.

I finished my freshman year, outgrew my anger and coped much better with the bully in my life.

I now had a new nickname, "Bull." It stuck for many years to come. My lack of self-confidence did little to match my responsibilities at home since my parents relied on me more heavily as the built-in babysitter. But life was good.

I would make up stories in my head while I mowed the yard or did other chores. I knew I wasn't going to be a farmer, though I didn't really know what I did want to do—except I wanted to go to college.

Meanwhile, Norbert, Linda and Nancy joined our family, and in 1973 I graduated from high school.

A brave new world was at my feet.

5 - MATERIAL THINGS

I hoisted the bale off of the loader, an innovative invention that made the hard work of putting up hay much easier.

It was the summer after my graduation in 1973, and Vincent and I had put up many a cutting of fresh hay in these fields for two bachelor brothers who were getting along in years.

Alfred Gorman, the youngest of Grandpa Roy's cousins, did what his older brother, Ed, told him to do. There was a pecking order. But Alfred was more of a socializer.

During one of our breaks, Alfred related the story of his military days in World War II.

"Ed wrote to the top brass and asked that I be given a hardship discharge after our father died. I didn't much care either way. I enjoyed what I was doing," he explained. "After I got my papers, I took a bus to Maryville, stopped at the local bar and closed it down. I then came home and I've been here ever since."

Ed was extremely shy and reserved. If you got a "yep" out of him, you took notice. Most times he giggled some.

The two brothers raised sheep and cattle, and the old farmstead was much the way it had been in the 30s and 40s, without any big alterations. After daylight savings time was implemented, the two brothers refused to change their clocks, or their ways. When we went to work for them, the hours were on the standard time clock.

Vincent and I got 10 cents a bale. Take that times 3,000 bales, times three cuttings a year, and that was $450 for each of us.

My mother and father let us blow a portion of that on fireworks. Our cousins Randy and Marty would stock up on a bunch of fireworks from a South Dakota fireworks company and so would we.

My father may not have hated the Fourth of July at our house, but he strongly disliked it. He couldn't get any work out of his boys on that day as we were enthralled with shooting off our massive amounts of firecrackers.

Only one rule prevailed. No fireworks until the Fourth.

My Uncle Rich and Aunt Darlene and all their kids would come to our house for homemade ice cream churned up the old-fashioned way, and we would have a colossal Fourth of July celebration that would put many town galas to shame.

The money we made from putting up hay for the Gorman brothers was an incentive to do hard work in those summer days, plus we would have some spending money through the year for going out on Saturday nights.

Vincent got there quicker than I did. As the oldest, I had to break through a lot of barriers with my parents. If you wanted to do something, you went to my mother first. She had been to high school and understood the dynamics of social circles, unlike my father who sometimes needed some convincing.

She was pretty much able to get the job done.

Not only was I responsible with the Gorman job, but I was also the one my parents relied on as the built-in babysitter. I didn't mind either. I'd inherited my Grandpa Roy's love of children.

As the sweat rolled off my brow, I hardly cursed the work because it was the last summer before college and the money was good. I was still living at home, and as far as planning for the upcoming months, I really didn't have a clue.

I was once again comfortable where I was and wasn't truly motivated to leave home as yet.

"Hey, Vincent, what's Ed doing?" I asked when I saw the old man drive the antiquated Farmall tractor toward us.

"Really not sure, looks like he's coming to tell us something."

"Well, keep driving 'till he gets here. It will take awhile." I said, and I hoisted a bale off the loader and placed it neatly in a slot on the load,

Vincent laughed and let out the clutch as we proceeded about our business.

When Ed arrived alongside our wagon, Vincent stopped briefly. Ed touched a bale and I looked on, puzzled.

"Did you want something?" I asked.

"Naw, not really. Alfred just got thrown by the elevator and is resting. The dogs are looking after him."

Vincent and I gave each other puzzled glances.

"Should we go see if he's all right?" Vincent asked.

"Oh, he's all right. You can go ahead and put up this load."

"Well, I think we better check just the same," I said, getting the sense that Ed wasn't really sharing with us how serious Alfred's situation was.

"Aw right," Ed said simply. Vincent and I hopped on the back of the old Farmall as Ed patiently and quietly drove it back to the barn.

Alfred was lying in the grass, and the dogs were hovering over their master in a protective way. I realized the man was in pain, and Vince and I jumped off the back of the tractor before Ed had stopped.

"Are you all right?"

Alfred explained he had simply tried to move the elevator from the barn, something he had done a hundred times before, but because he had lost some weight over the winter and wasn't as strong as he had been, the elevator had lifted him up in the air and deposited him without mercy to the hard ground below.

"Maybe you better get the car, Marvin," Vincent was saying.

"Um, yeah," I agreed, somewhat panicked. "Sure."

I had run a six-minute mile in high school track, never fast enough to do anything but come in dead last, but today, my legs had wings.

As I got out of the car to help my brother, we both attempted something we knew immediately wasn't going to work. We tried to lift Alfred into the car.

He uttered a string of profanities that caused us both to ease him back to the ground.

"We've got to call an ambulance," I said, stating the obvious.

"Oh no," Ed said. "He'll be fine. We don't need no ambulance."

"I really think we should," Vincent said.

"I'll be back," I said, and I rushed to the car and sped off. I wasn't waiting for Ed's approval.

I was glad Alfred had told me his story of getting out of the service. He gave me the impetus to not do what my elders told me and to rely instead on instinct.

When I got to the house, I rushed to the phone and picked it up.

"Well, you know, she went down to Condon Drug and got some of that yarn, but I do declare, it was not very good quality."

"Hello, this is Marvin Wilmes," I breathlessly interrupted the party-line conversation that was taking place.

"Well, I never –"

"Alfred Gorman is hurt and hurt bad. I need the line to call the ambulance."

Both women immediately hung up, and I dialed 911.

"Where is your location?"

Enhanced 911 wasn't a reality yet. The question frustrated me to no end as I had a vision of Grandpa Tuttle explaining where the Gorman field was. "Now, ya know, five miles east of the Gallagher corner, and then you go a couple clicks west."

"Listen, we're north of the intersection of Highway 136 and Junction N. I can meet you there and lead you out here. I can't explain how to get here. I'll be driving a blue 1967 Ford Galaxy 500."

"Sounds like a plan. We'll meet you there.

My father had surprised me with the car the summer of 1972. As older brothers go, I knew I fared a little better than my cousin Steve in breaking through parental barriers, but the greatest barrier had just been smashed.

The car wasn't a speed demon and today was no exception. I pushed the accelerator to the floor, and I raced to meet the emergency personnel. It was too far, much too far.

However, I arrived at the corner just as the ambulance did. I breathed a sigh of relief since I was halfway to my destination.

"Let's go," I said, and I jumped back into the car and led them to Alfred.

When we arrived, they immediately set to work at loading Alfred into the ambulance while the entire time, Ed protested the move, saying Alfred simply needed some rest.

Vincent looked just as exhausted as I did from worrying about Alfred's condition and listening to Ed's mantras about how we didn't need an ambulance.

Once we arrived at the hospital, the doctors determined Alfred had sustained a broken hip. At 72, that was a major setback, but he enjoyed the camaraderie and the care he received from his candy striper nurse, Aunt Delores.

Fork in the road

When I graduated from high school, I was following the advice of my business teacher, who proclaimed, "Become an accountant and you will have the world by the tail."

I wanted some of that. So my focus turned to accounting.

The economics class sunk my ship. I had no idea at the time that being tied down with a life of numbers was so diametrically opposed to the creative beat in my soul, which was as yet undiscovered. That would come much later when I wrote letters home and realized the power of the flow of words.

Oddly enough, as I would mow the yard, my mother would look out and see my mouth running a mile a minute. I was putting together a story. What a story world I created too. I would visit my fantasyland while rounding up the cattle, while taking a walk or walking the beans.

No one at my small high school saw or encouraged the natural talent I had. To even think for one moment that a Wilmes could be a creative soul? Sadly, I didn't have the confidence to nurture my own gifts.

I had the lead in our junior play, *Margie and the Wolfman*. All the work we put into it for one performance was fun. Yet, I never saw my creative strength as an asset.

My two masters were my father and Grandma Naomi. She was a schoolteacher and identified with me, many times taking sides with her perceptions about my pecking order with Vincent that were really never issues at all for me. However, as the oldest in our family, like Steve, I would later find responsibility boring down heavily on my shoulders whether it was put there or not.

Dad wanted me to work a year before I went to college, experience the world. Grandma would hear nothing of it. I ranked fourth in my class academically, dead last athletically. The school, my grandmother and my own ugly-duckling persona out on the farm pointed me in the direction of hitting the books.

However, I didn't know myself well enough to succeed in the transition from high school to college. The reality of having to work for a living also pressed in on me and I thought I could do both—work and go to school.

So, in the summer of 1974, I moved into a modest Maryville apartment and started work at Regal Textile, a factory that specialized in making disposable diapers.

By fall I had changed my major to computer science in hopes that I would somehow beat the fact that I was failing at the academic rigors of college. I couldn't let anyone know my grades were crashing, least of all my grandmother, as I struggled to find my identity.

Maybe that was why the glitter of the maroon 1974 Formula Firebird called to me. I was driving a simpler car that served me well. My father had given in to the pressures in the household to provide his oldest son with the 1967 Ford Galaxy 500 that had just enough get up and go to keep a high school senior out of trouble.

He may have given in to the more staid vehicle with the reasoning that my brother could drive it after I was done, but now I wanted this tempting apple of my desire. It would cost me $4,200, and with my father's signature underneath my own, it could be all mine.

I'll be the first to admit in hindsight that the car contributed to some delinquency on my part. After all, Grandpa Roy would later lament from his armchair position that some hooligan had cut "kitties" in downtown Ravenwood by the post office, and that person should be run out of town on a rail.

He had no idea that those "kitties" were mine and I wasn't about to claim them either.

I mean I had him and even myself conned that I was still the good kid. I didn't dare let one smirk slip from my lips, even though my blood pressure had risen to a level that had made me blush with embarrassment.

I'd been invited to come home for an appointment with the

salesman and my father. I walked into the farmhouse excited when I saw the Firebird parked in the driveway. When I saw the back of the salesman's head I knew that I had won the battle. I had an ally outside the family.

Dad puffed thoughtfully on his pipe, and it was obvious to me that my best defense was a good offense. You have to know when not presenting an argument is the best action to take. He looked like a man about to do something he was going to regret for some time to come, but in his middle-of-the road philosophy that I had grown to know in the early years of our relationship, he decided it was time for me to take some form of responsibility in paying for what I wanted.

The Firebird did that, I guess. It also made me very popular among my peers. Suddenly, I was the cool guy who was challenged to race on the Ravenwood bottom. It changed who I was.

Unfortunately, one Saturday night in September of 1974, I dropped David Severson off at his house in the country. My best friend, Dan Welch, was in the front seat and his brother Kirby was in the back. I had been driving somewhat erratically on the country roads. After we turned around in the driveway, I became even goofier while I teased my friends and floored the accelerator and dipped and scooped over the gravel hills.

"I'm putting on my seatbelt," Dan hollered, failing to hide his uneasiness at my dangerous behavior. "You need to slow down. This is insane."

Adolescence and a devil-may-care attitude sometimes combine to make a toxic mix. And so it was on this night. Kirby sat in the center of the back seat holding on to the back of the seats for dear life.

After all, I had maneuvered the blue Ford over the gravel roads with ease while obtaining emergency help for Alfred Gorman. I felt invincible and a little bit egotistical showing off my daredevil skills to my friends.

Once I turned east on the next gravel road, I decided to really give Dan a good scare. I confidently floored the accelerator again. Then, when I began to crest the hill, I suddenly realized I was going much too fast for the conditions. I felt the car leave the ground and when the wheels connected with the road again it was with loose gravel.

No control was to be had. I saw the ditch and the pole coming at me. I said a brief prayer of some sort because this was going to be the end. Fools die young, and I was going to be one of them.

Somehow, as we hit the ditch, the car landed perfectly in between the fence and the pole and in a nanosecond stopped cold.

Everyone was in shock and I immediately asked my companions if they were all right. Dan was already laughing, but I didn't see anything funny at the moment. Forget ourselves, my only pride-and-joy possession was really messed up.

I tried to back it out of its spot and the Firebird wouldn't move. The night didn't end with just one bad decision—we made another when we got my Uncle Joe's tractor out from his farmstead a mile away and attempted to pull the vehicle out of its hole.

What we failed to realize was that the impact had been so abrupt and so hard that the emergency brake had locked on, preventing us from being able to remove the vehicle from its spot.

We got David's father out of bed, and he took us home. As we drove into the driveway, my brother's silhouette showed up at the window first, followed by my mother's and then the dreaded one, my father's.

I was exhausted and knew I had to face the music. The next morning, Uncle Joe and Aunt Donna were at the farmhouse, demanding an explanation as to why I allowed someone else to use the tractor. Everyone understood that I was being punished enough because my car was smashed up in a ditch, but they punished me anyway.

It was to be the beginning of the end of life as I knew it in Parnell, Missouri. I was in the process of growing up, greeting the world.

The recession of 1974 was brutal. My coworkers and I feared showing up for shifts as a note would be on the door to say how many days we would be working that week. It went from four, to three, sometimes to as low as two.

My job was not able to financially support me anymore, I would become unable to meet my car payments and my friend Dan would pay me back big time for that crazy ride I gave him.

6 – THE ACCIDENTS

My entrance into the United States Marine Corps had spiritual overtones. At that time, I had come to the end of a dead-end path.

After wrapping my sports car around a pole, I continued to deny that I couldn't burn the candle at both ends and survive.

The fall of 1974 was a dark period for me. I chose to go to bed exhausted instead of attending my classes after I got off work at 8 a.m. My paychecks got smaller as work slowdowns affected my job. I was able to deceive my parents into believing everything was okay when I moved into the $60-a-month apartment

I was a failure at school, I continued a charade of attending classes and I refused to drop out. One afternoon, having left the television on while I slept, I awoke to Fess Parker roaming the wilderness as Daniel Boone and had a revelation that something needed to change.

I pushed myself to get up and get dressed with plans to go play pool with my best friend, Dan Welch, and as I left the apartment and closed the door, I suddenly had a still small voice whisper to me.

Things are about to change for the better.

I had no idea where this idea came from and actually would have discounted it as a random thought banging around in my head except for the fact this particular night was to mark a major turning point in my life.

I had accepted less for myself. I was trying to please both my father and my grandmother with the working-and-going-to-school fiasco while trying to live it up racing the Firebird in country drag races.

You cannot serve two masters.

When I walked into the basement of my friend's parent's home, he excitedly bypassed racking up for a pool game and slapped me hard on the back.

"I've been talking to a recruiter, Bull," he excitedly recounted, using the childhood nickname I'd earned as a freshman in high school, which still haunted me this many years later. "We can join the Marine Corps on the buddy plan and I can be a PFC right out of the gate."

My friend had come up with many lame-brained schemes before, but this was so way over the top, I declared him insane. His brother, Kirby, also joined the shenanigans, and he bet me a cool $50 that I would never do it.

Dan was very persuasive that night. He always was with me. I listened with attention; my interest was piqued, but I wasn't sure why he thought I would be drawn into such a plan.

I left Dan that night with the usual thought that, once again, he had crazy schemes, and once again, I would ignore him and move on with my life.

I was visiting my parents when the recruiter caught up with me via telephone, thanks to my best friend's persistence in wanting to get his stripe by signing me up. My mother, who had likely been up many a night praying for my soul, suggested I at least hear the guy out. I reluctantly agreed, having no intention of following through.

I had already been issued a semester suspension from the university. I had ranked fourth in my graduating class, so what was this?

I readied myself for the appointment, prepared to give this man the heave ho.

Was I that gullible?

Whatever he said in that half-hour was a lifeline to me at that moment. I signed his papers, committing myself to four years in the United States Marine Corps. It was truly on a whim. Nothing was binding until I passed the physical in Kansas City and signed up then, but I had stepped across the line.

Sometimes, I knew, when a Wilmes stepped across the line—nothing is going to change his mind. It was the German in my heritage.

I couldn't explain what I'd done to anyone. I believed this was a good move for me. After all, my current life was a shambles; work had slowed down, the car payments were killing me, I had failed college.

This was a chance to turn things around.

My father stood at the bottom of the steps when I announced to my parents what I had done. I had seen that stance before. I had sensed that apprehension before.

The year was 1962, and he was declaring that it was time for him to move on.

His jaw was set. He was silent in this moment now.

"Four years, that's a long time."

I had no idea what he was envisioning in his mind's eye when his eldest son announced he had joined the military. He himself had spent two years in the United States Marine Corps. Two years had been a long time for him.

He had a right to be uneasy about my decision. There was no backing out of this commitment. Just two years before, I'd thrown a fence post into the back of a wagon as I jumped for joy at the announcement coming over the radio.

"President Richard Nixon has rescinded the draft."

I had escaped Viet Nam, war and the cursed military.

So why was I the one riding on the bus toward Kansas City while Dan Welch continued doing his daily chores on the farm?

I had no idea that as my parents saw me off at the bus station, my grandmother would hold my father accountable for what she termed a foolish decision, and my mother would run around the corner and mourn the loss of her son.

The difference between my grandmother and my mother was that the latter had the courage to know it was time for me to leave the nest and to let go.

Later that night, at 2 in the morning, as I joined many of my peers in the pits of basic training, I believed I had made the biggest mistake in my life. But there was no turning back now.

There was only survival.

The ultimate denial

In 1975, while I was in Marine Corps boot camp, two tragedies occurred in the Wilmes family when Uncle Tom's wife, Penny, and my cousin Steve were each killed in separate accidents two weeks apart.

When my mother called to tell me of Penny's death, I was affected, but not as deeply as by the news of Steve's passing.

Steve was Aunt Dee's age, the eldest of the next generation. I had to break many overprotective barriers with my own parents, but Steve's were made larger by the events of 1963.

He was killed in a fatal car crash at the age of 23 and left behind a wife and a son.

Like his brother's death, this news numbed me for its basic cruelty.

At the time of my cousin's death, I had been stationed at Camp Pendleton, California. I was a Marine Corps recruit in the second phase of boot camp. I was working on the maintenance crew on that June day in 1975 when I was called out of the field and my presence was requested in the main office.

Puzzled, I dutifully responded.

I stood at attention in front of the drill instructor who was my taskmaster.

"PFC Wilmes reporting sir," I obediently stated.

"At ease, soldier." The hardened Marine's features softened as he walked over to me.

"I have bad news, Wilmes. Your cousin Steven was killed in a car accident. My condolences to you and your family."

The news bounced off me with such a force, I instantly forgot all military protocol.

"What?"

"You can call your family now. You also have the option to go home if you need the time. I can't guarantee you'll be reassigned to this platoon, but you'll be able to pick up where you left off."

I had no chance to digest any of this. The Corps had stripped me of all sense of emotion and home seemed a foreign place. In that instant, I knew one very important fact.

If I broke this cycle, if I went home, returning would be hard after tasting civilian life. My platoon was my family now. I had made it this far, I wanted to go the distance.

"Sir, I'll be all right if I don't go home. I want to graduate as soon as possible."

The drill instructor eyed me curiously. A shadow of respect passed across his face as if I had surprised him with my resolve.

"Are you positive?"

"Yes, sir." I stared straight ahead, still digesting the news.

"Okay, carry on."

As a Marine I made the decision to stay. As a cousin I failed to walk through the valley of the shadow of death and the bereavement process. With Steve's death, I was now the oldest living cousin of the George Wilmes lineage.

When I returned for leave between boot camp and my next duty station in Millington, Tennessee, besides greeting my brother Roland, who'd waited until I returned from boot camp to be born, I failed to support my cousin Alan—or was I even able to grasp the loss for myself? Steve's death was a statistic to me. I discussed it with my mother and father on the way home from the airport, but in boot camp I had been in an emotional vacuum.

Bernard and Cecelia were my godparents. I had no clue how to even acknowledge to them they had lost another son. I never uttered one word of sympathy or recognition of the fact when I saw them and I also behaved the same way with his brothers and sisters.

I simply hadn't processed Steve's death or taken it in fully.

For me, his death had occurred in another universe

One evening, while out on the town, Alan was quiet and reflective. I allowed the thick weight of the silence between us to hang in the air. I didn't know how to comfort or to support my cousin, so I simply reflected with him. I had no words.

Steve had been haunted throughout his life by that fateful day in 1963 when he watched his brother drown. I knew he had. It was something I always knew in my heart, and it was his cross to bear in this life.

I had no idea of knowing or even relating to the fact that Steve and I had so much in common in terms of responsibility as the oldest sons in each of our family trees, but that commonality would be magnified in the future.

In 1975, I left my role as older brother and babysitter behind and began my adventure as a young soldier of fortune.

Steve's was a cross of responsibility for his brother's death; mine would later become a cross of responsibility for my siblings and family.

I simply came home and refused to talk about Steve, just as my mother had reprimanded me not to talk about Elmer.

It was now second nature to me.

While I was stationed in El Toro, California in early 1976, Steve's sister Georgia wrote me a deep spiritual-seeking letter that I never responded to.

Fact was, I didn't even know how to answer my own questions about our place in the universe, let alone advise my cousin on such matters.

My military travels in those first couple of years took me to San Diego, California, then to Memphis, Tennessee, then back to California at the El Toro base and back across the country to Beaufort, South Carolina.

I was a 20-year-old Missouri farm boy who had landed smack dab in the middle of life in the real world. I loved the variety and I loved the adventure of it all.

My Firebird once again got me in trouble in the fall of 1975 as a roommate borrowed it and wrapped it around a pole in downtown Memphis, Tennessee.

My military friend Jerry Clark and I had been scheduled to pick up our dates in Galloway, Tennessee, and instead we were playing detective trying to track down my wheels.

While we were involved in this search, both of us were irritated that our evening plans would have to be cancelled, but also I felt frustrated at not knowing what had happened to my car.

As we were still trying to figure out how to solve that crisis, I received an emergency message from the corporal on duty to call home.

I composed myself, determined not to let my mother know about the missing car.

"It's Dan," she said on the other end.

"What happened?" I gasped as I visualized a tractor tipping backward and rolling over my best friend.

"He has cancer."

The word was one that was completely foreign, especially that night.

"Vincent was with him when he collapsed. His feet gave way underneath him. They went in and had to amputate his leg."

I still had no idea that denial was something I was getting better and better and better at. I took in the news, coped with its bitterness, not recognizing that our friendship had already begun deteriorating.

I was changing within the military. I had stepped outside the small world of Parnell, Missouri, and I would never be the same again.

"We get what we need in life, not what we want," the words of another military friend would guide me in later years.

Yet, it was so true.

My appointment with destiny would be on the motorcycle owned by Jerry Clark on our way to Disney World in Florida from Beaufort, South Carolina a year later.

Our scheme was simple. Drive both the Firebird and his motorcycle down, stop off in Zephyr Hills, Florida to visit his aunt and leave his bike there for storage. I told him in no way would I get behind the wheel of his motorcycle.

Looking back, I can see no logic in the plan. Why I agreed to it, I have no idea, but the decision would dramatically change my life.

After stopping at a Georgia restaurant to eat, Clark claimed he was exhausted and would I please take over his bike. My friends were always making demands on me that were impossible. Once Dan had insisted on leaving the Iowa State Fair in Des Moines to go do his chores an hour after we had arrived.

So why did we just drive two hours to get there?

I reluctantly agreed with Jerry, just the way I did with Dan, because I had no choice.

As I donned the helmet and was ripping down the interstate, I remember thinking to myself this was a big mistake. The wind whistled all around me and my body became tense.

As I approached an interstate exit, I took a deep breath and began to ease into the turn. Panic began to overtake me when I realized I had made a terrible misjudgment and had entered the exit far too fast.

I attempted to slow down, but anything I tried only made the situation worse. I knew in a split second that I was losing control of this monster machine.

My life literally flashed in front of me.

God save me.

Lena Logan's words were there before I even had a chance to form them in my mind.

I felt a wind gust blow the bike sideways. I wasn't quite sure what was happening, but my body flew over the handlebars. My head hit first and my body skidded across the pavement.

My first thought while I lay there was, I'm alive.

I looked up. My heart sank when I saw the Firebird round the bend out of sight. My friend didn't see me. I then looked over at Jerry's broken bike.

"Are you all right?" A man had stopped to come to my aid. I slowly rose to my feet, sensing with dread my friend's reaction to the bike's demise, but again I pondered the fact that I was alive.

After the man comforted me, and more activity took place and the police arrived, Jerry eventually returned to the scene of the accident having noted I was no longer behind him. The first thing he saw was his bike suspended in the air by the tow truck.

"Oh my God, I've killed him."

I do believe God's hand had answered my prayer, gifted to me by an elementary religious education teacher.

Refusing to seek medical treatment, I would regret that decision the next day as every bone in my body ached.

However, nothing was broken, we arrived at Jerry's aunts' who let us know through her body language that Jerry could of at least called before showing up at her doorstep.

We spent the next day at Walt Disney World and as we sailed across the water towards the Magic Kingdom, I felt pain in every bone in my body after the shock of the accident wore off, but I was fortunately okay.

The miracle I perceived would precipitate an examination of my life and my search for God in the ensuing days and lead me to return to faith in Jesus Christ.

Not even Jesus promises a rose garden, but he does promise us a life and a life we can live more abundantly.

The truth came to me in the form of Hal Lindsey's *The Late Great Planet Earth.* I threw the book against the wall at one point, realizing that I could never live up to what it asked me to do.

I only needed to pick up the book and continue reading, which I did. I was stunned. I came home to God in the summer of 1976 and since then, despite all the valleys and the mountaintops, God has never abandoned me, even though I may have abandoned him.

I experienced a spiritual rebirth that was beyond anything I had experienced in my prior 21 years on earth. It would pit me and my father against each other on the subject of religion, but that didn't matter.

Within that core truth, the process was born. I later discovered that the book was only an entryway into my Christian rebirth. God uses many paths to call his children to him. In 1976, it was my time to come home.

Lean not on your own understanding.

God wanted me to deal with a lifetime of denial, eliminate it and learn from that.

Thankfully, my mother was spared knowing the full details of the motorcycle accident. It wasn't exactly one of my most stellar moments and not one to shout from the mountaintops, but I became a true advocate of motorcycle helmets as I believe wearing one saved my life that day.

One year later, my Uncle Ken would almost die after a motorcycle accident, but God had more work for him to do too.

7 – A ROSE BY ANY OTHER NAME

If you love something, set it free. If it comes back to you it was meant to be. If it doesn't, it never was.

Jesus Christ came to give us life and to give it more abundantly. In the arena of relationships, I came to learn the truth of the anonymous quote that would guide me in 1980.

I would also come to learn the truth of the Romans, 8:28 bible verse: *All things work together for the good, for those who are called according to his purpose.*

As a young Marine, I was one of those who didn't find my soul mate right out of the gate. I had too many adventures that kept getting in the way. My first love was cheered on by my uncles when I rode the bus as a sweet second grader. Many years later, I was involved in a "relationship," which meant being a part of a triangle.

I gave away my class ring, envisioning years of happiness ahead. The visions of sugarplums, however, were in my head, not born of reality, but out of infatuation. When I finally accepted the unattainability of the object of my affection, I would later look back on the experience as one that ended exactly as it should have.

Yet, my father, who believed he was the expert on affairs of the heart, gave me a fire and brimstone lecture covering his favorite topic for his teenage boys. "There are other fish in the sea. Come on. Why tie yourself down now?"

I didn't believe my father could appreciate that I was in love and I couldn't understand why he couldn't because, after all, he modeled love every day with my mother.

My father was overprotective, and I resigned myself to having to pay that price as the oldest son.

When I entered my last year in the Marine Corps, I learned that our squadron would be going overseas for a six-month deployment to Japan.

My anticipation of going to a foreign country was interrupted by a phone call from my brother Vincent.

"Joan and I are engaged," he said into the phone. I couldn't have been happier to hear the news. "I'd like you to be my best man."

"Congratulations. I'd be honored to be your best man, but we're scheduled to go on a six-month deployment to Japan. We leave in April and we won't be back until late October."

I heard a pause on the other end of the line while I regretted being stuck in the Marine Corps as things were changing rapidly back home. The differences between my brother and me were more magnified since I'd enlisted in the service.

"Well, I guess we have no choice but to wait until November."

"I really hate to have you do that."

"We do what we have to do. As long as you promise to be home then, we'll make things happen then."

"Well, okay, I guess we're on. Man, this is great news. Thanks for calling."

Once I hung up the phone I felt somewhat melancholy as I realized so many things were happening back home without me. My cousin Alan was getting married in August and I would miss that one because of the deployment.

The year was 1978 and in the relationship quadrant I didn't have much room for one. But a certain Ann Krang, a Korean woman, had occupied some of my time while I was stationed in Hawaii.

She was 25, worked as a cocktail waitress in a Korean bar in Honolulu, and together we planned and schemed many adventures of our own.

"I plan to follow you to Missouri," she would say. "We make a good future there."

Both of us kept our walls up as this was a relationship of convenience. Life held too many uncertainties for me to be tied down at this stage of the game, and I had learned to play the part of a rolling stone quite well.

Prior to my leaving for Japan, my friend Jim LaLime and I had started to talk about taking a trip to Maui together. We had both heard it was a paradise to behold and up until now we had just spent time seeing the sights of Oahu.

As the weekend approached, we gathered in the hangar of VMFA 212 with the rest of our Marine brothers and our hearts fell as Sgt. Major Atwood told us about the lockdown of leave prior to our departure for Japan.

"No Marine shall take a weekend pass," he sternly ordered. "We may be called at a moment's notice and we have to be ready to deploy."

Jim and I looked at each other in despair, seeing our Maui plans go up in smoke. But Jim was determined; he called his boss aside.

"Marv and I were planning on going to Maui for the weekend. Isn't there any way we can go?" Jim pleaded.

Fortunately, Jim's boss had a soft spot and explained to Jim that we could go, but we both had to check in with him every eight hours. Jim eagerly agreed, and we were amazed to find ourselves on a plane to Maui.

We'd been working seven days a week, and the luxurious paradise of Maui, as opposed to the commercialized Honolulu district and the military environment of our Marine Corps base, made for an ethereal experience.

Against my better judgment, Jim talked me into taking our rented car into the more underdeveloped part of the island, and on our way, we came upon a peaceful scene of a church nestled alongside a beach with several horses grazing nearby.

Both of us felt we were touching something higher than ourselves, and the experience transformed our friendship as well as our attitude prior to leaving for Japan.

I stood on a cliff overlooking the pastoral scene below me with the wind blowing in my hair, feeling a sense of surreal peace.

In this moment, I came into union with my creative and inner spirit. I knew who I was and the sense was one of incredible destiny.

It was a sign of things to come.

Japan would change our lives forever.

Friendship Day

I can honestly say that when love came to roost on the shoulders of a best friend while we were stationed for six months in Japan, I had a front row seat.

This occasion was the second time I truly saw love flower in front of my eyes, and I know God gave me the wisdom to be a counselor. Kind of like the bridesmaid who is always in the wedding, but never the bride, I was going to be in my brother's wedding after we left Japan, and my own romance clock was ticking and always going off, whether it misfired or not.

I had always stumbled across red herrings in the path when it came to love, but in 1978 some cultural experiences were turning my view of the emotion upside down.

May 6th was Friendship Day on our base in Iwacuni, Japan and Japanese citizens descended upon our military installation. This day was one when cultural walls were torn down and the memory of August 6th, 1945, the historic day that America dropped the atomic bomb on Hiroshima, Japan, was drowned out by a truce called by both American soldiers and Japanese countrymen.

A mutual Marine coworker in our squadron, Terry Ireland, couldn't wait for us to meet his friend Naoko and her friends.

So, when the introductions first took place, I was taken aback that Naoko started talking to me, and one of the other Japanese girls started walking with Terry. I was perplexed, to say the least, because the two barely acknowledged one another.

Then something magical occurred. We had a changing of the guard, and Jim and Naoko settled on each other. As I conversed with the girl beside me and struggled with her broken English, I glanced behind to see how Jim was doing.

He and Naoko had fallen way back and were engrossed in gazing into one another's eyes and lost in conversation. I was thankful Jim had found a connection, but in turning back to my partner, I simply rolled with it, still aware Jim was having a connection that I had never made before and that wasn't happening here either.

Three months later, I was by Jim's side as he struggled with the tensions of his relationship with Naoko. True, we were in a different culture, but I had seen this one other time in my life. That was when my brother Vince was looking at two pictures side by side, trying to make a decision of the heart. He could no longer remain with his former girlfriend.

A new woman, Joan, had captured his heart. That had been three years before; now in November, I would witness their union in marriage.

Lovestruck

I knew my Marine Corps brother had found his pot at the end of the rainbow. He was in love. It had happened at first sight. It'd happened in the first half-hour.

However, Naoko's family didn't look kindly on the relationship due to the historic consequences of the American bombings of Hiroshima and Nagasaki on the family.

Jim sought my counsel on this situation many times, and I always tried to encourage him, but I could see the culture was his barrier in making his dreams come true.

Then came my blind date, which just like on Friendship Day, resulted in no attachment. The girl Naoko set me up with didn't speak a word of English, or so it seemed, and even though we attempted to connect, we had to mutually give up. We were able to pull together enough communication to each let the other know we wanted to end this. We met up with Jim and Naoko, and my date left on the next bus. I was relieved that the ordeal was over.

I had no idea that Naoko had other ulterior motives for bringing me along this particular night.

As Jim, Naoko and I talked on the street corner, another bus pulled up, Naoko reached over, thrust a letter into my hand and said, "Thank you for being his friend. Take care of him."

I was stunned. Jim looked at the letter I was holding, and his face went ashen. I watched Naoko's face as the bus drove away.

I grabbed Jim's shoulder. "Let's go sit down, have some sake and talk about this."

His shoulders were already shaking, and he broke down in tears. I felt literally helpless as I tried to piece together and understand what just happened.

When I sat across from my friend and read the crumpled letter Naoko had handed me, I immediately saw the truth, not only in the letter, but also in the anxious eyes of a frightened Japanese girl who'd fallen in love with this Marine.

I knew in that instant that for Naoko, there was only one Jim.

"Jim," I said with a resolve that I had previously not known. "Naoko didn't write this letter."

He looked at me in disbelief, about to correct me by saying it was her handwriting.

"Her brother or somebody else was standing over her as she wrote this letter," I continued. "She wrote it under duress. Yet, she found a way to still say she loves you."

"What does it matter? What can I do about it?"

"I saw a look in her eye. She made the decision against her will. I say, go after her."

"You really think so?"

"Fight for this."

I was scheduled for a 72-hour stint on wheel watch, so it would be some time before Jim and I would get back together to compare notes on my advice.

I finished reading the short novella *Jonathan Livingston Seagull* that Jim had given me to read. He said that I was Jonathan and he was Fletch in the birdlike parable. Japan had changed us both as a spirituality had followed us here that sometimes made our military brothers think we had drunk too much sake.

Why did I believe so strongly in this union destined for failure as the deep, dark past of Hiroshima and Nagasaki made Naoko's family disdainful of any American?

Through another's eyes

A month before, I had gone with several friends, including Jim, to visit Peace Park in Hiroshima, but after becoming fascinated with the museum, somehow I got separated from my companions, which didn't make me feel too comfortable. I knew very little about how to maneuver my way back to base from this sprawling Japanese city.

I was sitting by a park bench cursing my bad luck when a young Japanese man in his early 20s sat down beside me, and wanting to practice his English, struck up a conversation. I was somewhat annoyed, but I played along anyway.

"Why did it have to happen?"

His question pierced the very fabric of my American pride. Indeed, why did it have to happen?

"I just came out of the museum," I said dryly. "I didn't know that every country was racing to get the bomb first. It just happened to be us."

"Yes, I know, but why did it have to happen?" He got up and started walking. "Come, follow me."

I was intrigued by the simplicity of his curiosity about the question and his persistence in asking it, but I wasn't prepared for the mural he wanted to show me: an artist's rendition of many Japanese souls wailing in the aftermath of the bomb's landing in their world. It was a painting depicting hell itself on August 6th, 1945.

We stood in one of the most peaceful places on earth I had ever been, aptly named Peace Park. The dome of the building located at Ground Zero was all that remained as a concrete memory of that fateful day.

"I don't know," I said to him. "I guess no one really won. I just believe it ended the war."

His eyes sad, he continued to practice his broken English and he eventually detected my distress at not being able to locate my friends.

He offered to help me get home, riding the train to his village and then explaining how to get back to the Iwacuni train station.

He was gone from my life as quickly as he came into it, almost like a thief in the night, an angel catching me unaware as a piece of America's history touched me in a way that no history book could explain.

The advisor

The 72-hour shift was non-eventful as plane after plane landed with wheels down. I was always at the ready in the small shack at the end of the runway, but the story of Jonathan Livingston Seagull intrigued me and kept me awake.

I wondered how Jim's reunion with Naoko might have gone, and when I ended my shift, I wearily went to my bed and fluffed out the blanket as the note sailed in the air and gently wafted to the floor.

Puzzled, I picked it up to read the short message in my friend's hurried handwriting.

"I had to go to work today. Naoko and I stayed under the bridge last night. She's here. Could you make sure she's okay until I get off."

Here? I peered around the row of lockers toward Jim's space. I saw a blanket hanging over the entryway. Surely not?

"Hello," I said nervously as I knocked on the metal locker.

"Yes" came the timid female voice from the other side of the blanket.

I entered while Naoko presented herself as the frail and scared Japanese girl she was right now. I had to get her out of here before she was discovered.

"Well, how about we go get a Coke or something. The PX is about a mile from here. You don't mind walking, do you?"

"No." She put her hand to her mouth and giggled.

Our journey was somewhat awkward as we walked side by side in silence. When we passed each young Marine, I would either say, "How's it going?" or they would say, "Hi there."

I had no idea the impact this was having on my female companion. All I could think about was how insanely in love Jim must be to have sneaked Naoko on base and into the barracks. I was coming to the conclusion that there was no hope for him.

I followed through on my promise to buy Naoko a Coke. As I settled in the seat across from her, once again her hand went to her mouth.

"I am so ashamed. We did something so stupid last night. We stayed under the bridge," she said.

I looked her in the eye, taking in the newfound resolve to keep this love fire burning I saw in her.

"I've always found in life that sometimes you have to take a stand for yourself and do what you think is right, no matter what anybody thinks," I said.

"Thank you," she said gratefully. "I am so glad you're Jim's friend."

I leaned back and took a long sip of my Coke. I couldn't help thinking how lucky Jim was to have this love in his life.

I suppose I was somewhat jealous and also somewhat tired of

my own call at the moment to single life.

At the end of our time here, Jim would volunteer to stay behind for another six month deployment, and the couple would leave Japan with plans to marry and with Naoko's father's blessings.

All is fair in love and war and Jim and Naoko's love was a testament that love can break down the highest walls and strongest barriers.

As St. Paul would attest, "And the greatest of these is love."

I was glad to have had such a pivotal role in keeping their love fires burning and I knew I had been God's instrument in achieving that end.

7 - EARTHQUAKE

Standing in front of a packed church, I pulled at the knot that held the rings of the bride and groom in place.

Then I gasped in horror when the groom's ring fell from the safety of the pillow and fell to the carpet on the church floor. From there, it not just landed, but bounced, and when I bent to retrieve it, my new sister-in-law's nephew was in the way.

"Blake," I whispered to the boy in desperation. "Can you move your leg just a bit."

The entire episode of retrieving the ring likely lasted less than 45 seconds, but it just as well could have been 45 minutes.

Hardly anyone noticed, except for me.

The morning had started out chaotically enough.

The cattle had escaped from their fenced-in pasture and Vincent was having to chase cattle on his wedding day.

Absurd.

My little brother was getting married. I couldn't have been happier.

But storm clouds had risen over our happy family since my brother's marriage was met with more than a little opposition from Grandma Naomi.

According to her, they were too young. It would never last. And the strain that my mother went through during this period was intense.

I felt as if I had been absent during an important evolutionary cycle. My grandmother's fears were all grounded in her idea of a perfect order in which things should happen.

After all, I was to be the first to get married, yet I was still single. This was all wrong.

"Hi, I'm getting ready to fly out of here next week and I look forward to seeing you," I excitedly relayed to my grandmother when I called her from Hawaii.

"They have a job for you to do."

"What?" I asked. "What do you mean?"

"They have a job for you to do—best man. You aren't going to do it, are you?"

I pulled the phone from my ear and looked at it in dismay. No one loved my grandmother more dearly than I did, but what was this?

I felt as if someone had taken a knife and stabbed me in my heart. I had no clue this was going on while I was away.

"Yes, I'm going to be best man. I'm proud to do it."

My grandmother's voice was tense, stressed. Our conversation was short and concise after that. We ended our talk quickly, then I nervously dialed my home number.

My mother answered the phone in her usual cherry way.

"What's going on?" I asked, forgetting pleasantries for the moment. "I just called Grandma, and she was totally down on Vince and Joan's wedding."

"I know. We're beside ourselves to figure out what to do," Peggy said. "She has this idea they're too young or whatever."

"Because I'm not married first."

"Something like that. It's not your problem though." I recalled a letter my mother wrote recently about it being a burden to be an only child. Now I understood the source of her anxiety.

"I'm sorry this is happening," I told her.

"So am I," she said.

I had mixed feelings over dumping my frustrations about my grandmother onto my mother. I felt better afterward, yet I knew it was a heavy burden for her.

As for me, I was one who always fought for the underdog, and for some reason, this favoritism shown me and negative comments about my brother had emerged more obviously since I'd joined the

Marines.

Many times I argued with my grandmother over the issues she had with my brother Vincent, but they weren't my battles to fight.

Yet with each dagger she threw in that direction, I felt the pain in my heart, not so much for Vince and Joan, but for my mother who was always stuck in the middle.

The big event

I had a large conflict of interest when I came home for my brother's wedding on November 4th of 1978.

Grandpa George and Grandma Gertrude were celebrating 50 years of marriage on January 6th, 1979, exactly one month before I was to be discharged from the Marines.

Everyone was going to be there. Cousins, aunts, uncles, every last descendent planned to be at this event. I had to be open and frank about it.

It was too close to the wedding and also too close to discharge. It would just be insane to try to make it, let alone afford it on my military paycheck. So I told everybody I would be the only one not able to make it.

"We've been talking about it, and we think you should try to make it," my mother said one evening as we were gathered with our coffee cups and sat catching up on all the local gossip.

"I can try to get off, but man, it will cost a bundle."

"We'll take care of it," Alfred said.

"You mean – "

"We'll pay for your ticket."

I sat and calculated the jet lag from flying back to Hawaii and then in another month flying home again for only three days, and I decided it would be worth it.

"I'm in."

Fork in the road

I had to do some wheeling and dealing with my bosses to get the time off to fly back to Missouri for three days, but they liked me just enough to let me talk them into it.

Staff Sgt. Hamilton had another agenda in mind when he cornered me one day.

"So, you're going back to Missouri?"

"Yes," I said.

"You know it won't be easy."

"How so?"

"Things will have changed back home. Friends will have moved on, and you'll be a stranger in your own land. Plus, you'll have to fend for yourself. Here you get three square meals a day and have a roof over your head every night. You can save yourself the hassle and reenlist."

"Oh no," I protested. "I want nothing to do with that."

"Why not?" he asked. "Just think about it. We want you to stay."

I stared Staff Sgt. Hamilton in the eye as I realized he was making a serious pitch.

"You're serious?"

"As a heart attack."

"No," I said. "I'm really not interested. A chill ran up my spine, and I realized I had just made my first civilian decision.

Family matters

I closed my eyes and tried to force sleep as the flight to the States was a redeye. I was becoming adept at airport etiquette and style, but sleep wouldn't come on this flight.

There was something magical about the miracle of what was happening. I had departed Missouri, leaving everyone but my parents with the assumption that I was going to be the only descendant not able to attend my grandparents' 50th anniversary.

To not attend didn't seem right on many levels, but Vincent had scheduled his wedding for November 4th, their anniversary was January 6th and I would be discharged February 4th.

Four years before, my life had taken a dramatic turn. Since then, my brother Roland had been born the summer I got out of boot camp, and the youngest, Karl, had surprised even my mother when she attempted to deliver the news to me in Yuma, Arizona while I was on deployment in November, 1976.

I had volunteered to stay back with the detail crew for VMFA 212 to finish packing up and departing from the deployment, thinking I would enjoy another night of liberty.

That was not the case since the top brass assigned me to man the phone for the squadron. I was disgruntled to say the least, but I had no choice except to obey my orders.

As I was engaged in my pity party, the phone rang and I half-heartedly answered.

"Lance Corporal Wilmes speaking."

I heard a long pause on the other end of the line.

"Marvin?"

"Yes." I perked up at the sound of my mother's voice.

"Go ahead, Ma'am. I guess this is the party you were trying to reach."

"I didn't expect to get hold of you," she continued. "I have some news. Karl Roger was born."

"That's great," I said, and I suddenly realized my selfish desire to get one more night of liberty in Yuma had resulted in my manning the phones at the opportune moment of my mother's phone call.

I would later label this type of coincidence as a God wink.

I could feel God's smile surround me and I gave up my funk for the rest of the shift and the rest of the deployment.

On the plane bound for my grandparents' anniversary celebration, I turned restlessly in my seat at the memory.

I thought of Steve and Elmer. I was now the oldest second generation descendent of George and Gertrude Wilmes. It was an honor I didn't relish, but one that made my absence from the celebration less than desirable.

When I changed planes at the Dallas-Fort Worth airport, my insomnia only increased. I was beyond sleep at the anticipation of surprising my grandparents.

As I entered the reception hall of St. Gregory's Catholic Church, my grandmother was beside herself the moment she spied me entering.

My grandfather looked on and didn't say a word, but his temple pulsated. As my father related later on, Grandpa George wasn't much for emotion, but no doubt he was deeply moved by my act.

I observed my mother's happiness at having pulled off this surprise. Family was her number one priority, and she worked hard to keep my father's family together. She was a social shaker and mover.

"Marvin got homesick again," my Uncle Rich teased.

"Yep, Marvin is one of these jetsetters, flying to Hawaii and back every other week." Uncle Jerry laughed while he sipped on a cup of coffee.

I took the teasing, but the fact was that prior to coming home for Vincent's wedding, I'd researched staying in Hawaii.

But November's trip had taken that pipe dream out of my head. I was a jetsetter. I had flown on many airplanes and had been stationed in Millington, Tennessee; El Toro, California; Yuma, Arizona; Beaufort, South Carolina; Kaneohe Bay, Hawaii; Iwacuni, Japan and Cubic Point, Philippines.

Staff Sgt. Hamilton knew a little bit of what he had said to me because I was about to experience culture shock of momentous proportions.

Love's sting

The wind was whipping the snow around the roads while I squinted through the whiteout and kept time to the cadence of the windshield wipers. This was actually happening, and my heart was pounding. Nothing could keep me from my destination.

This reunion had been months in the making. I had been out of the service for a year, and I had taken it upon myself to believe that miracles could happen in my life as well as anyone else's, and in Jesus's words *if you say to that mountain, move, it will be cast into the sea.*

Incredibly, that had happened. All of Regina Raul's resistance had melted just like nothing, but many hurdles remained to jump in bringing her from the Philippines to the States. I could only imagine the culture shock she would feel once she stepped out into the cold tundra of Missouri's winter as opposed to the tropical havens of her home country.

Regina and I had met shortly after Jim and Naoko pressed through their barriers of love. I had resisted this deployment to the Philippines with every fiber of my being. It was only for three weeks and my best friend had no desire to go, either.

Nevertheless, the orders did come through and we couldn't escape the trip to yet another foreign country. Since Jim and I had deepened our Christian faith together, I reasoned that we must have a reason for going.

I knew the temptation awaiting me, and with little opposition,

I fell into that enticement shortly after landing in the tropical paradise. Despite my pledge to resist going off base, I found myself following the lead of my cohorts and I magically discovered myself escaping curfew with a beautiful Filipino girl who had this huge painting of Jesus Christ in her living room.

I was swept up in the enchantment of her tales of marriage and following me to Missouri, and this goddess giddily made fantasy plans while she cuddled up next to me.

I remember lying there in bed staring at the portrait of Christ and asking myself what I was doing here. In the bright light of the next day, she accompanied me back to base, and I observed an army of men and their escorts walking toward the main part of town.

I attempted to put on my best face of cheerfulness, but inside, I felt like a fake. At 23, I was too old to be playing this game. I knew this cheap woman would never follow me to Missouri, nor did I want her to.

We were literally two ships passing in the night, as corny as that sounded, and I was quite relieved when we parted ways. She knew I had already closed myself off, and I knew I couldn't live a lie. I had witnessed true love with Jim and Naoko, I was going to be best man in my brother's wedding in November and I knew what I was searching for wasn't what I had found.

The deployment to Japan had brought many changes to the people I had come overseas with. It brought out sides of people that I hadn't seen before. Jim's and my spirituality had lifted up and flown high with the grace of Jonathan Livingston Seagull.

And now I had cheapened it with a fling my first night in the Philippines. I was perfectly set up for a love affair that could make or break me.

I sought out one of my married friends who was keeping his vows by not being tempted by an off-base pass. I shared my distaste of the night before with him, and he shared with me the need for a movie mate, so we did something that made us both feel good—and stronger—we shared a movie night.

The next night, Jim and I reunited and decided to hit the club on base. We both had our reasons for wanting to hide from the world. Like the Adam of old, we wanted to cover ourselves and hide away.

When I saw her, I was instantly mesmerized. She was taller than most, slender and hauntingly beautiful. Our eyes locked from across the room, and she smiled. I smiled back, forgetting all resolutions I was making to myself at the moment.

"Hi, my name is Regina," she said, and she drifted to our table almost as if on a cloud. "Can I get you something?"

"I'll have a rum and Coke," I stated, almost mute with wonder.

That's how the conversation started, but we ended up spending hours that night talking about our families, our hopes, our fears. We were both from large families. She was the oldest of eight and was taking care of her father.

We laughed, we shared many tales and I found myself inexplicitly attracted to her on a whole new plane. My fear of the deployment being three weeks too long, over the next week turned into a hatred that it had to end.

Because my deployment was so short, Regina made the decision to distance herself from me in the last week. I took the rollercoaster ride with her, and when I felt the C-130 lift into the sky and fly toward Japan, a piece of me had been left behind.

For the first time in my life, I had touched the garment of love. Love had been returned, but had retreated in order not to be vulnerable. Unlike the first night when I had given my body, I had given my heart and it was wounded.

I was able to close that chapter in my life, finish my deployment in Japan, return to Hawaii and eventually travel on to my brother's wedding where I fumbled with the wedding ring and searched for it at the feet of the ring bearer.

The bouncing wedding ring reminded me of my love life. I dated a hometown girl for a time after I was discharged from the service, but my mind kept going back to that hauntingly beautiful face and that magical time.

I did the unthinkable. I reconnected to Regina by phone. She was stunned by the phone call. We exchanged several letters over the summer of 1979, and in one I took the leap. I asked her to marry me.

Miraculously, she said yes.

And now, here I was, driving through a blizzard to meet up with my fiancé. As I made my way into the airport and parked my vehicle, my mind raced with how this meeting would go. My last vision of Regina had been a look of sadness while her friend swept her away, preventing her from saying a proper goodbye.

I wasn't really sure what I thought when I stood there awaiting her coming off the plane. Yet, when I saw her face, the same joyful radiance seemed to shine forth, and I approached her to embrace and kiss her. She, in turn, lifted the plane ticket she had in her hand, hit me lightly over the head with it and said, "hi."

I stood there dumbfounded. Following to assist her with her bag, I felt the coldness of our connection was just as frigid as the air outside. Then, as we drove through the hills of snow, I sensed the culture shock she felt.

She kept talking about my buying an album, the Commodores and their song "Still." I thought it a very odd request, until I listened to the song on my stereo. The song musically recounted two souls that had drifted apart, and even though the flame of their love had extinguished, it was what it was and an ember was fast going out.

When I left her in my apartment that night and drove to my parents' home, I somehow knew the end had just begun.

And like a lot of other things in my life, I silenced the still small voice in my head with denial.

Sail on

Three weeks later, I stood at my bedroom door demanding to know from the woman who had consumed another three weeks of my life why she had even come.

The standoff was a turning point. She dialed the telephone, speaking her language, Tagolag, into the phone to her sister who lived in Colorado. That only infuriated me more. I had staked so much on this relationship, had believed that I could overcome any mountain, but sadly had only chipped away at the iceberg.

My mother had reasoned that we should both sit down and seek the counsel of a priest she had called. Oh great, I'm trying to save a relationship and you want to bring in a priest.

As Regina was also Catholic, she agreed, and that gave me some hope that all wasn't lost.

However, as the priest thoughtfully pressed tobacco in his pipe and talked to each of us about life paths and other matters of maturity, he turned to me and asked, "So, do you want to work on this or do you want to walk away?"

Suddenly, the answer was welling up inside me with such force, with such vibrance, I couldn't really believe how good uttering the words made me feel.

"I want to walk away."

Regina's answer was the same. The priest made a speech about how these interactions can turn things around for us, and I might decide to seek out the religious life some day. But I wasn't in any sort of religious mood at the time. I was trying desperately to make sense of my life at this moment and I just wanted to get on with the broken pieces of my life.

When I bought the ticket to fly her to Colorado and to say goodbye, the weight on my shoulders lifted.

My grandparents drove us to the airport in the longest car ride ever and Grandma Naomi, who had never been much for a Filipino granddaughter-in-law in the first place, said, "We were all praying that things would work out the way they were supposed to."

"I guarantee you they have," I answered. I hit the dashboard of my grandfather's car and said, "Drive on, sir, This is indeed the first day of the rest of my life, and yes, all things great and small work together for the good of those who love the Lord."

My grandfather broke out in guffaws of laughter, so I also laughed and Grandma shrugged her shoulders from the backseat.

I really did feel good and I was learning how all things do work together for the good, although I would need many years to actually fully realize the wisdom of those words.

A few days later, I was lying on the couch in my living room, feeling somewhat sorry for myself. I had left the Commodores album on for an extended length of time, long past the song "Still." I never really had taken the time to listen to the last track on the album.

Slowly, the words edged into my consciousness, and my heart jumped at their meaning. I stared in disbelief at the stereo and I reset the track. Then I danced around my apartment and God lifted my soul upward as Regina had unwittingly led me to buy the album that had *my* song on it.

"*Sail On*" became my freedom song. Many men had foolishly taken the path that I had. I was 25, a quarter of a century old and still floating free.

I suffered through a family wedding where I felt like everyone's eyes were boring into the back of my head, but that was more in my imagination than reality.

It would be a long time before I loved again or trusted the way I had this time. My faith grew stronger; God kept encouraging me that all was not lost nor was life an ala carte buffet where we pick and choose everything we want, just the way we want.

A childhood friend and distant cousin, Celia Bartram, was going through her own struggles and issues in the summer of 1980, and as I contemplated dropping out of school, she sternly scolded me that if I quit college, I would never go back.

As I approached September of 1980, I was mulling over how I was going to take on the many creative challenges of the remainder of my college courses while working fulltime when a crazy, creative, but very workable scheme began to form in my mind.

Simplify your life, and get on with it.

A still, small voice from God, or a plan hatched out of desperation?

I believe it was too radical to be the latter, especially since it worked.

I sold my 1979 Grand LeMans back to the car dealership, paid off the loan in cash, took the remainder and bought a blue 1974 LTD Ford with 115,000 miles on it right off the lot for $1,000 cash.

I made arrangements to get out of my $260 per month College Gardens apartment and traded down to a $90 per month house apartment on the second floor. I gave notice at my factory job, arranged to take on more hours at KXCV, the college radio station, took on more hours of college work per semester and experienced the biggest creative explosion of my life over the next two years.

When I drove up to my parents' farmhouse in the 1974 blue bomb, my parents were left speechless.

I knew what they thought, but they listened intently and both took a deep breath.

But I know for a fact my mother thought I had gone plum loco and probably blamed it on Regina.

She would have been right. Earthquakes shake up and rearrange the landscape. In this case, it would turn out to be just what the doctor ordered.

May 8th, 1982, I graduated from Northwest Missouri State University and then hit the drought of another recession.

Obtaining a college degree was one thing; finding a job was another.

9 - THE C WORD

The icy cold hands of loneliness engulfed me as I huddled up against the heater in my two-room cottage in Hobbs, New Mexico. But even the sweetness of the potpourri of Christmas candies including divinity, peanut brittle and buttered popcorn gave me little to cheer about Christmas, 1983.

Record cold temperatures and higher-than-average snowfall were making it a winter to remember.

Some of those I worked with had made wise investments in the stock market and in the black gold, which provided them with a decent living. They viewed their radio career as a sideline, something of a toy to tinker with.

I had accepted the position to serve as a starter block for my career, but the reality of the situation was I was barely scratching a living out of the barren desert land.

I called home to convince myself that I had a place to return to someday. I had chosen to follow the creative road in response to my calling in life, and so far it had paid little in dividends.

Staff Sgt. Hamilton might have been right. I might be on a fool's errand.

I was 28, torn between the struggle to establish my independence and getting past the recessive economy. I had served four years in the United States Marine Corps and come out a better and stronger man because of it, even with a testament of Christian faith that I probably wouldn't have found in my backyard. With that experience tucked away, I had a dream and decided that I wanted to major in communications.

After leaving my fulltime job at the factory behind and diving into the last year-and-a-half of my studies, the creativity in my soul exploded.

I was thrilled when the KHOB opportunity arose, 900 plus miles from my homeland, which was itself not distressing. I had sailed into unfamiliar territory in the military, but with all the essentials taken care of. I had survived within the Marine Corps fishbowl, but now I was in the ocean and everything about my life at the moment seemed like a misfire.

I had arrived in April, eager to begin my first fulltime radio job. It fulfilled many of my requirements, except for one, putting an adequate amount of money in my pocket to survive.

I failed to calculate the cost of the move, the starting salary and a higher cost of living. Wiser men would have counseled me to pass on the opportunity.

I still had faith in God and my home connections. At Thanksgiving, I had learned my mother had been hospitalized to remove some fibroid tumors. In her normal, lighthearted way, she shooed away the alarms going off in my mind. She was the one keeping me up to date with her letters and news from home. It was those same letters that made being miles away from my roots easy.

The letters had stopped coming in September 1983. This should have given me pause to wonder if something might be wrong at home.

I had also brushed aside my mother's farewell when my parents had visited me over the summer. A look in her eyes that seemed sad I attributed to her sadness at having to tell me goodbye, that this move had been more permanent than previous ones.

"You take care of yourself," she said. "Give me a kiss."

This was completely out of character for my mother. We weren't a very expressive family, and I sensed something was on her mind.

My father fidgeted when we exchanged our farewells. This was also odd, but denial of reality was easier than allowing my mind to run away with worry.

"Hello." My mother's cheerful voice on the other end of the

line made me push down the paranoid worries that occasionally plagued me.

As she updated me on all the goings-on back home this Christmas, I could detect the stress in the background voice of my grandmother, and as the pauses got longer, I knew Mom wanted to tell me something. I patiently waited.

"Marvin..." She paused again before delivering the news. "Aunt Rachel died last week," My eyes closed, and I let out a small sigh of relief. So this was the source of the tension.

My mother's aunt had suffered at the hands of one of the most horrible diseases I had encountered—multiple sclerosis. I barely remember the vivacious and lively Rachel of my childhood. The last time my family and I went to see her in Parkville, Missouri, she was bedridden and her body was disfigured.

Though her body was wracked with pain, I had never seen anyone with such optimism and cheer. I saw the love of her husband, Edward, as he spun a wild story about her visitors, and she laughed while he gently wiped the saliva from her mouth.

I perceived great courage and optimism in the spirit of a woman who had nothing to live for except the joys that surrounded her with her own family. It was not in sadness that I greeted the news of her passing, but rather in thanksgiving as I knew she no longer had to suffer.

I hung up the phone, attributing the nervous tension on the other end of the line to the loss of another loved one.

My faith had sustained me in Hobbs, but I was living in poverty, and Hobbs was doing little to sustain my faith. I had signed up with a head hunter company to assist me in my job search, and the bounty for their finding me this job was 10 percent of my first year's salary.

As I thought of my younger brothers and sisters at home, I prayed that God would use me in my lifetime to help them find their way in the harsh, cruel world when they reached adulthood. I had been a third parent of sorts, since my parents readily put me in charge of babysitting when I arrived in adolescence.

I had little to be merry about in Hobbs. God seemed distant.

The first holiday tragedy occurred when the cyst on the back of my neck continued to become irritated and eventually couldn't be ignored anymore. I realized it had become infected.

The second one occurred when I went to pick up my monthly paycheck.

"I'm sorry," the owner's wife said as she handed me three bills. "This is all we can pay at the moment."

I stared in disbelief at the two 20s and one 10-dollar bill. After I filled my car with gas, I would have little left for food, and nothing for rent.

Two weeks earlier, I had asked for a payday advance to replace the alternator in my car. My boss was more than willing to provide me with the help, but gave little indication that things were as bad as they evidently were.

I was beginning 1983 broke, desolate and in bad need of a miracle.

The owners of KHOB promised to pay the rest in a week when more ad revenue invoices were paid. Meanwhile, the doctor gave me the bad news that my infected cyst would have to be surgically removed. With no insurance, I would need to pay him in advance.

I would have to call home and ask for help. I also knew I was going to have to retreat, regroup and try to find another job, because I wasn't sure KHOB was strong enough to keep operating—let alone whether I had enough resources to survive my living situation.

Humbly, I called home for the money for the procedure. This wasn't what I had envisioned when I'd followed my heart's desire to major in communications.

All things do work together for the good for those who love the Lord and are called according to his purpose. Had I lost my purpose? What was God trying to tell me, and where was he?

The creative gene

Peggy's favorite book was *Little Women* and she used to revel in the adventures of its main character, Jo.

I had discovered my own writing muse in the military and learned my mother could also write letters chronicling the everyday events back home. This connection was one of understanding and of comfort to me. At times, I felt as though my mother was the only one who truly understood my own creative spirit.

"It's hell to be creative."

I had spat out those words to my mother on my maternal grandmother's front porch in Ravenwood, Missouri as I expressed my frustration at not yet finding my way in the world. My mother silently absorbed my statement, knowing the inner struggle that was mine to live.

She merely nodded.

Even though I had been raised on a farm, everything about my life was in such opposition to my inner creative calling, so much so, that it sometimes blocked the confidence I needed to be who I felt I was called to be.

The prodigal son

The telephone call home deflated my pride. Out of my conversation with my parents, due to the unpredictability of my employer's financial situation, they encouraged me to come home for vacation to regroup, which meant they would have to send more money for a flight.

I still hadn't resolved my inner doubts about why Mom's letters had quit coming, but the third holiday disaster was the short, curt note from my mother that accompanied the check from my parents.

"Nineteen-eighty-four will be a new year. Prayers that it will be a better year for everyone."

The ominous tone of the note unleashed a barrage of worries. What was going on? I actually allowed my mind to formulate the possibility of one scenario that didn't comfort me. Were Mom and Dad having trouble in their marriage? It seemed an unlikely conclusion, but my sixth sense had picked up on something being wrong with my parents.

I was now imagining the worst. My isolation in Hobbs, New Mexico didn't contribute much to any rational thought connected to the cryptic letter.

I gave in to my impulse to call home. My mother answered the phone, and my fears only intensified. Her voice was strained, and this call was most unwelcome.

"What are you calling for?"

I was at a loss for words, but I struggled to find my voice. "I was just wondering how everything is with you."

"I'm fine." There was a long pause on the line. "Did you get the check?"

"Yes. I get the cyst removed on Friday."

"Good luck with that. I'm really busy right now. We can talk when you get home."

As I hung up, I came to the conclusion that my mother and father were definitely having troubles in their marriage, the only thing that made sense. I put together the pieces of former conversations and the reality of Dad's running away from something only loomed larger in my imagination. I still hadn't come to terms that there might have been a more serious issue.

I concentrated on removing my infected cyst. As the surgeon numbed my neck and sawed away at the intruder, I imagined my life being disposed of in much the same way. I had no present and no future. I only had God.

The pain in my neck was unbearable once the Novocain wore off. I tossed and turned on my couch, which doubled as my bed. I prayed to God to relieve the pain.

The phone interrupted my pity party.

I answered it as my sister-in-law Joan's voice came through on the other end. Like my mother, she wasn't in the mood for much conversation.

"Your mom has cancer."

Four words that rocked my world. There must be some sort of mistake. My first thought was about the seven kids still at home. God could not be that cruel.

My selfish bout with pain ended with that one sentence. Cancer meant death, didn't it? It had taken my mom's cousin-in-law Orville, it had taken a young girl named Anita, it had taken a classmate named Donna and it had resulted in the amputation of my best friend's leg while I was away in the service.

Joan had informed me the surgery was scheduled for the day of my flight home.

Things were moving so fast, I hardly had time to meditate on the reality that this was a coincidence beyond human comprehension.

I'm hardly keen on patience, and when I checked into the Dallas/Fort Worth airport, I dialed the hospital and asked for an update. Joan came to the phone.

"Your mom came out of surgery about an hour ago and everything went well," she reassured me.

She offered no further details as she curtly ended the conversation.

The phone call had done little to comfort me. All I could do was continue my trek home. I didn't feel confident that 1984 was going to be that better year my mother had talked about.

Denial's child

I'm from a generation that grew up watching the TV show *Twilight Zone*, a surreal journey into fantasy and science fiction. The feeling that I was in a real-life episode was only enhanced when my father and my mother's parents greeted me at the airport.

We had two hours for them to share with me the results of the surgery, what was going down in our lives and how we were going to deal with this. I was amazed that all three were strangely silent on the subject of my mother.

In the way I had been trained to do all my life, I followed their lead.

Only by the grace of God was I able to refrain from broaching the subject. I sensed that if my mother were brought out as a topic of conversation that both grandparents would be lost in a sea of emotion. Their only daughter had cancer. That burden was enough. Their silence gave me the sense that the news couldn't be good.

I was beginning to accept the reality of my mother's mortality.

My grandparents excused themselves after my father parked in the hospital lot. The sound of their car doors slamming had barely faded away before my dad turned to me.

"It's not good," he said, and he shook his head in bewilderment. "It has spread too far. Doc gives her two months. Grandma and Grandpa are taking it hard. She doesn't know yet."

"I see. I'm so sorry." We had just driven two hours in an enclosed vehicle, and no one had the decency to tell me until now? How was that possible?

I was numb. I took the car keys from my father since he was going to be staying the night at her bedside. I would go home to meet my brothers and sisters. Tomorrow was another day: I would see her then.

As I walked up the sidewalk to the familiar two-story farm

house, I heard a ruckus inside. I entered the porch and rounded the bend of the short flight of stairs to the kitchen, the same one where the news of my cousin's drowning was delivered 21 years earlier.

The scene before me made me howl in laughter. My brother Norbert, clad in a night-robe, was holding the oven's light housing on one end. My brother Dean struggled with the other end.

"Help," Norbert said, and his laughter intensified.

"What in the world?"

"Just help," Norbert said, and the laughter continued to make it more difficult for him to hold up the fixture.

"You dork," Dean teased. "We were fighting and Norbert slammed into it."

I shook my head and went to the aid of my two brothers. Life had provided a lighter moment where one was needed. We were all laughing.

Laughter was better in that moment than for us to do what we couldn't give ourselves permission to do.

Cry.

10 - RESPONSIBILITY CALLS

The family gathered at St. Francis Hospital. This vigil was something we weren't accustomed to. I was sitting next to my father, as my grandfather sat beside me a defeated man, shoulders slumped, and tears welling up in his eyes.

My mother was his only child, the middle child of three, and the only one who had survived. The details of my uncles' births and deaths weren't mine to know, but Mom was spared their fate and lived. Despite being an only child, she wasn't selfish, and she was always the first to sacrifice. I thought I knew a lot about my mother, but this year I would learn much more about her faith and character on a deeper level.

"So has the doctor told her yet?" I asked my father who was holding up extraordinarily well despite the circumstances.

"No, he told us that she doesn't need to know yet." I observed a firm resolve and anger in his facial expressions that made me think he wasn't totally convinced he should follow these particular doctor's orders.

"Is that a good idea?" I asked. "How can you fight something if you don't know what it is?"

"I know. I just hope he tells her today. It would be easier on us." My father glanced toward my grandfather, and I silently thought I would want to know if it were me so that I knew what I was dealing with.

This was our problem, looking back over the years and

through the goblet of history. Doctor knows best: Follow his orders. Patient advocacy was something foreign to my parents, even though they had nine children.

Our family was insulated against tragedy and sadness in our own lives, though we knew many who had walked a road of sadness.

My parents had never suffered the loss of a child except through miscarriage. I recalled the worried expression on my mother's face when my father rushed her to the hospital in the fall of 1974 after she excused herself from a Friday night get-together with Raymond and Bert.

"Your mother will be fine," Bert assured me while I anxiously looked on.

I smiled at her, knowing that this would be a season of loss for my mother as she would likely lose the baby.

Now, I was still recovering from the shock of the cancer diagnosis, and that was because I hadn't experienced the days and weeks that led up to today with my parents.

In some ways, my mother had protected me. I pondered the absence of her letters since September. Had that been the beginning of her period of worry, and she found not writing easier than tempting fate and revealing all wasn't well with her?

I dutifully stepped into a supporter role for my father and didn't question the family doctor's decision to keep her prognosis from my mother.

We all gathered outside my mother's hospital room as my father quickly dispensed the order that we not let on to her about the terminal nature of her illness. We were there to put on brave faces.

We filed into her room, my brother Vince and his wife, Joan; my mother's parents; me and my father's mother, Grandma Gertrude. We stood at the foot of her bed and assumed our cheeriest smiles.

My mother's eyes trailed along to gaze into her father's.

She began weeping and put her hand to her face. I turned to see where her gaze was locked, and I saw my grandfather's tears streaming down his face. His emotion couldn't hide the truth. My father, my brother and I were telling the lie with precision, but my grandfather couldn't.

He was losing his little girl. He was losing his only child. He was losing his world.

We had no words to say. My father threw a string of expletives against the doctor after he left my mother's bedside. I was beside myself that the truth wasn't being told, but we had just told it in spades. The doctor was wrong in having us try to pull off this deception.

"I'm going to demand he tell her," my father said.

I nodded agreement then I went to my grandparents' side to comfort them.

Our family as a unit went through a metamorphosis that morning. We stared down the enemy, which was cancer. The doctor gave her two months.

We weren't willing to accept that diagnosis.

We would soon learn that neither would my mother.

Call to action

"Martha said she can't believe we're here." My mother's head had gone into her hands again in 1982 as she wept. Just as she had collapsed at our kitchen table in 1963 upon hearing the news of my cousin Elmer's drowning and fallen into my father's arms at the news of Aunt Odelia's passing in 1969.

Her parents, my father, my brother and his wife and I were seated in the family Suburban ready to drive to the Parnell cemetery to bury Orville Durbin, the husband of my mother's cousin, Martha. Our faces were somber as we took in my mother's grief.

Orville's passing from acute leukemia was a shock, but cancer and illness were not strangers to the Al and Eunice Madden family. Martha's niece, Anita, had been struck with cancer and fought a valiant fight for years before succumbing to it.

Orville had operated his own bulldozer and was a man of quiet strength who had been felled by this beast, and in Orville's case it had been the treatment, not the cancer that he had succumbed to.

"I can't believe we're here" was exactly how I felt now.

I believed in God. My faith was grounded in a personal relationship with Jesus Christ, but my life had been beset by storms as I was tossed about on the sea. Where was the man who walked on water when I needed him?

This just didn't make sense in God's timeline of destiny. From the beginning, my first thoughts were, *But who will finish raising my seven younger brothers and sisters?*

They ranged in ages from David, who was turning 17, to Karl, who was 7.

Nineteen-eighty-four was to be a year of great miracles and also one of weak faith. The miracle that was to manifest itself wasn't the one desired, nor would it be the one expected.

Once Mom was moved to a room, I joined my father at her bedside.

"There is something we want you to talk about," my father said, again boldly taking charge of the situation, but this time with a gentleness that I rarely witnessed. For a moment I saw the young man pondering the nine years he had lived near my grandparents and preparing himself for the independence from his father's influence.

"You said things weren't working out in Hobbs," my mother whispered.

"Not exactly." I put on my best face of defense. "I don't know if the radio station is going to survive. Frankly, I'm kind of in a rut."

"We're going to need help." The words floated out of my father's mouth. "I can cosign for a loan for you to come back home and help out. Of course, you could look for another job."

My dad, the proud man that he was, was humbling himself to ask me to save him from the responsibility of his younger children during this crisis of need. My parents were turning to the babysitter of the family to come home and protect the household from ruin.

At 28, I wasn't where I wanted to be in life. It would be a sacrifice of my dreams and my career, but in my heart I knew God was calling me home. I had the experience of KHOB on my resume; maybe a regional radio station could use my talents.

I gazed into my mother's eyes.

"What do you think I should do?"

My mother said not a word. She simply resigned herself to a nod of her head.

The battle to fight Goliath was on; the peace of the decision lightened my heart.

All things work together for the good? As a family, we threw the two-month prognosis over our shoulders. The war had begun.

"It is not over."

Much activity took place around our farmstead, but not the kind that would be expected. Some of my aunts from the area rallied to descend upon my parents' household and conduct Operation Deep Clean.

A sense of nostalgia took place as each took part in this community ritual of healing. None of them could do anything to keep the beast at bay; cancer was something that hadn't roosted in the backyard of the Wilmes legacy until now.

Observing this from afar was Father Regis, a priest who first towered tall in my mind as a man of incredible faith that most mirrored my own. My father and I tangled over the issue of religion many times in my youth, and 1984 was not going to be an exception.

I had been called back to the Catholic faith as a Christian, which set my father and me at great odds. In his mind's eye, those who never struggled with faith were the chosen ones. All this nonsense that Jesus freaks preached was for those who wanted to live for today and never give a care for tomorrow. My father believed this religion was the religion of the me generation and it had no value in his ordered world.

Why did I always park myself at the end of the couch for the weekly after-church debate where teen and father battled among the ruins of modern-day issues? He loved the fire of the battle, and though I always ended up leaving the arguments with a red face filled with anger, I evidently got something out of the banter as well.

It would always begin the same way. I would bring him his coffee, put mine on the stand between his chair and the couch and sit. He would invariably puff on his pipe and say, "Here you go, read this," as he shoved the latest *Sunday Visitor* magazine into my face with the article selected that he was convinced would raise my ire.

I would read it and instantly take the more liberal view while he would take the conservative one, and my mother would look on in dismay as we slashed out at each other with raised voices and firm convictions. I simply defended youth, the underdog and whatever the opposite view of my father's opinion was at that moment.

Years later, after I came to my own personal faith in Christ, my father was a testament to it because he would constantly challenge me, and I would defend it to the core. He would argue all the reasons I was wrong. My mother always ended up refereeing the argument, getting us to see that essentially we believed the same thing, but we each had a different way of getting there.

I was unaware that my mother's faith, as strong and stable as it was, came late in her life as a result of marrying my father. Which only enhanced my long-held view that faith arrived at later in life is sometimes stronger than faith avowed forever—but nonetheless they spring from the same roots.

The truth of the cross is that anyone who affirms true Christian faith and believes that Jesus Christ is the central tenant of that faith has met Jesus Christ on his own road to Damascus.

I would later ask myself in the aftermath of 1984: Was that the road we were on?

Father Regis had been the one who confidently walked out on the altar of our small Parnell parish and announced to the sleepy congregation before him at Orville Durbin's funeral, "It is not over!"

Instantly, I was transported back in time to the 13-year-old boy holding the cross at Aunt Odelia's funeral, wondering what in the world everything was about anyway. I felt the Holy Spirit well up inside me and a tear form at my left eye now as I knew the priest spoke of Orville's coming resurrection in Christ.

This man of God spoke with such conviction that I knew it was not over. The man who stood before me was a new kind of priest, a priest I would need during this crisis period in my life.

What I failed to recognize was even priests have their 40 days in the desert, and Father Regis would be no exception. He had developed a deep friendship with my mother since she was the head of the parish catechism program.

Water in the desert

My aunts came in force to clean the house from top to bottom. My mother was still recuperating from her major surgery and the time fast approached for me to return home to Hobbs. I had made the decision to leave. A weight had lifted off my shoulders, and I was adjusting to the news that my mother had metastasized colon cancer that had spread to the liver.

She wore an ostomy bag, a reminder that the disease was not kind. Aunts had whispered that Mom had given out statuettes of the Virgin Mary for Christmas with a tear in her eye.

Mom had known for some time that something was wrong. I wasn't privy to all the concerns she had or the doctor's appointments leading up to the diagnosis, but the cancer had been in her body for several months before it was discovered.

The two-month prognosis had long ago been pushed to the back of my mind. My mother's courage in the face of her illness encouraged me. Our family didn't focus on the time left; we focused on treatment.

Her resolve was that she was going to beat this thing, and the seven kids at home fueled her commitment.

After I flew into the Midland, Texas airport, an ice storm was the first obstacle to getting home safely. I drove my dark-blue LTD Ford across the ice-glazed roads for the 100 miles to Hobbs. It had carried me far in the last three-and-a-half years.

This wasn't the first time I'd been in an ice storm in an odd place.

One of those greeted me on my drive from visiting a Marine friend at the Yuma, Arizona base back to my freedom base in California on a February day in 1979 where I would get my papers to civilian life. At El Centro, California, I was detoured north when the interstate was closed. As I weaved my way north and west, I passed a jackknifed truck, and then I found myself in the mountains. I was creeping along at 20 mph, and I needed to inform the base that I was going to be late.

I talked to God on that winding trip because not only did I not have communication, losing control of my vehicle could mean careening off the side of the mountain. This was one of those surreal moments when you can't understand how you got where you are.

I longed to find a gas station, town or anywhere where I could place a call and let them know I was on my way. How ironic, being AWOL on the date of honorable discharge.

When I saw the phone booth nestled alongside the mountain

road, I couldn't trust what I was seeing. Surely, this couldn't be, with no civilization for miles. But of course, that's why it had been put here, for people who were in the same dire situation as I now was.

Or a mirage created by God.

Either way, I eagerly made a call to the base and clarified my predicament. The sergeant on the other end of the line explained that everything would be all right, told me to take my time, be safe. He had no reason to believe I was lying to him as this was about getting my discharge.

Now, as I was returning home from Missouri and continuing to creep along at a slow pace on the ice-covered Texas roads toward Hobbs, the temperatures outside eventually rose enough to melt off the glaze. I was never so happy to see the cracker box of a house when I drove into the driveway.

I heard the water gurgling as if from a nearby creek. Oddly, there was no creek. From underneath my house, a river of water flowed, making a mud pit in the back yard. I unlocked the door and entered to witness water spewing from the kitchen sink. The pipes had frozen and broke. Everything in the house was soaked from the deluge.

Strangely enough, I stood there and laughed as a madman would.

"Anything else?" I challenged to the air. "Honestly, anything else?"

Silence. God wasn't going to answer me just now.

Nineteen-eighty-four wasn't going to be better as my mother had hoped; 1984 was going to challenge every ounce of faith I had. If I had ever expected an easy path in life, I now knew it wasn't going to happen at this moment.

My survival instincts kicked in. Accepting that this was just another obstacle in the road helped me rise to the challenge, and I sought to find the water turn-off and went about setting things right. I called the landlord to ask if he had noticed the water problems. He admitted to knowing about the problem, but he assumed I would call him if I needed help.

I rolled my eyes, and I patiently explained to him I had been gone for a week.

They say that laughter is the best medicine for what ails you.

There was plenty of that while I cursed under my breath, at the same time with this prayer on my lips: "Lord, get me out of this God-forsaken pit."

I was reminded of Corrie Ten Boom's words from the movie *The Hiding Place*, which had come to me at a particularly distressing time in the military. "There is no pit deep enough that He is not deeper still."

Yes, but how deep do you want me to go?

11 - THE CRUCIFIX

The crucifix that became a permanent fixture of my mother's clothing throughout her illness became legendary for me. I discovered the letter detailing its origin among the large number of get-well messages my mother received shortly after the bad news made its rounds in northwest Missouri and beyond.

What was most striking was the pure volume of well-wishes from people whose lives Mom had touched. I was about to enter into an annoying period, however, which was also endearing in a way.

"You must be Peggy's boy."

"Yes I am."

"Oh, your mother was such a wonderful person. Why she...." And then they would relay the special connection that they shared with her.

After I returned home from Hobbs, New Mexico, I wasn't sure what I would find when I drove up to the farmhouse. The last time I'd seen my mother, she was bedridden in the hospital and slowly regaining her strength with the goal of returning home.

I walked up the sidewalk toward the porch and was startled.

"Boo." My mother playfully jumped from around the corner, and the angst that was on her face the last time I saw her had been replaced by her joyful radiance.

She always had a way to convey that everything was going to be okay,.

The priest's gift

Of course it wasn't. Was this denial played out? Our family was to go through a very challenging year, which would affect us in so many different ways. My Aunt Dee would later put a spin on my first radio job adventure in New Mexico.

She explained that if things had been wonderful, if it was a good experience, it wouldn't have been so easy for me to leave.

"If things had worked out and were really going gangbusters, you never would have been able to pull up stakes and just leave," she told me. "God had a plan. It wasn't time for things to work out there as your parents needed you now."

My parents were a topnotch team together. Mom had never been anything except a housewife, but that had changed in the prior few years once my younger brothers, Roland and Karl, entered school. Activities in the church began to take more and more of my mother's time, and she became a very much sought-after volunteer.

It was this leadership position in the church that called many priests, nuns and laypeople to her bedside during this trial.

Father John was one of those priests.

The young priest had presented my mother with a crucifix with a letter explaining its origin and intent. While I read the letter, I was moved by angst in the young man's words, as obviously he had experienced deep pain when he underwent his own faith crisis.

"I was given this crucifix at a crucial crossroads in my own life," the letter stated. "The person who gave it to me explained that he was given the crucifix when he was in crisis and was encouraged by the person to pay it forward by passing it on.

"I was moved by the gesture, and in time my crisis was resolved. Someone had bothered to lift my spirits with the gift of the crucifix, and now it's my turn to pass the crucifix on to someone who needs it more than I."

That person was my mother.

What crisis had Father John experienced, I wondered. Imagining an array of choices wasn't hard, as I could identify with a 20-something's yearnings for answers in a life that sometimes seldom made sense.

A crucifix is an ornament that can be worn intermittently or always, but it is a symbol of suffering, of Christ's death on the cross and the defeat over death through resurrection.

What impressed me most about the crucifix was that I rarely if ever saw my mother without it pinned to her robe, her nightgown, her blouse or whatever during her illness. The crucifix was not only a symbol of hope for her, it was a testament of faith, and it became a part of her during her intense journey through the valley of the shadow of death. Cancer had landed in our back yard. No one outside of our household really knew the courage nor the fortitude that Mom had put forth against this alien force in her life.

"I will beat this."

She definitely meant that from the fabric of her soul. After all, she still had seven children under her roof, and she didn't dare believe that God had granted her the miracle of their birth without giving her the ability to raise them.

From the actions of babes

I was in Hobbs, New Mexico when my nephew Craig was born. He was born in November of 1983, near the time of my mother's first surgery.

His older sister, Renee, had made a huge impact on me in many ways. I was in college when my brother Vince called with the news of her birth.

"It's like someone took a two-by-four and knocked me alongside the head," he laughed as he reveled in his new role as a father.

One spring day prior to graduation in 1982, with the final weeks of college work bearing down on me, I drove out to the farm where my mother was babysitting Renee. I had a lot of irons in the fire, and I was worried about several things like bills, a college paper that was due and where I was at this particular juncture in my life.

I had done things backward. I had gone out and seen the world in the military, and now I was hitting the books to make a future for myself.

I had decided to take a walk with Renee, who was no more than a toddler. I hoisted her on my shoulders and set out on a hike through the pastures and fields of our farm. She enjoyed this extra attention from her uncle as much as I enjoyed showering it on her.

We arrived at the back fence line of our farm near the north pond where the cattle were allowed to roam. I stopped at the gate and sat down while Renee began to play with pieces of dirt and bunched-up clods of dirt.

Something magical suddenly overtook me when I observed her simple play with the pieces of dirt. She moved them one by one and methodically was creating nothing in particular, just engaged in the moment.

As I watched her play in the dirt, it came to me that I was so concerned about the worries of this life that I failed to take the time to enjoy the simplicity of the world around me.

My niece was teaching me the wisdom of just being, without needing to be anywhere.

It was a rare moment frozen in time. Against the backdrop of an entire lifetime, it had no value unless you looked for it and decided to find it.

That day, I knew I had found something unexpected. That moment, everything just was.

For the moment, that was okay.

Second opinion

As I continued to sift through the large volume of cards, I found myself reading notes and letters of encouragement, and learning stories I'd never heard about my mother's life. She was coming alive for me in a way I had never known before.

News of Mom's cancer had shaken many people, and they responded by reaching out to her with card, verse and written notes of prayer.

The news of her illness was still surreal.

The details were matter of fact. The reason her situation was dire was because the cancer had spread to the liver. Dad and Mom were doing everything the doctor told them to do.

Up to this point, all cancers were the same to me. A cancer diagnosis just meant things were grim, but the stages, the different treatments and all that were foreign. As a family, we were uneducated about the disease.

My mother unwittingly was introducing me to patient

advocacy, something that was to affect my future career in dramatic ways.

Almost one month had gone by since the doctor had given my mother the grim news. I drove her to the doctor's appointment, where she was hoping for the referral to a radiologist in St. Joseph, Missouri. My father had come into town that morning because he had taken another vehicle in for servicing at Moore's Automotive.

My mother was still holding supports at arm's length. Her independence was important to her. Today, she would temporarily give it up.

I sat in the car, and my Mom bravely went into the appointment herself. I passed away the time by listening to the news and music on the radio. I was still oblivious to the support my mother needed since we always followed her lead on these matters.

She was always the one supporting us, not the other way around.

Some time went by before she came out to the car. She got in and grasped the steering wheel with her hands. Her voice wavered, but the fire of resolve was burning brightly in her eyes. "We have to go get your father."

I immediately perked up and realized that something had occurred in the appointment that no one was there for.

"What's wrong?"

She had done it so many times before. Stoically sucked it up, but this time she couldn't.

"He asked me if I had started taking pain pills yet." Tears welled in her eyes. "Can you believe it? He just gave up."

The cruelty of the comment took me a bit to absorb and realize the impact fully. Our deeper instincts of survival kicked in, and that was the day we sought a second opinion and went to an oncologist in Kansas City, Missouri.

That was the day we reclaimed Mom's comfort and life and spared her from a much deeper suffering than anyone could ever imagine.

That was the day we changed the two months to more than that, despite a doctor's pride in not referring her on, and the additional time was more valuable than gold itself.

12 - CANCER SUPPORT

In all sadness, there is joy; in all joy there is sadness.

Many truths were embedded in the events of 1984 for our family, but that one has most guided me through the rest of my life.

It is a profound paradox when you think about it. While positive events do cause us to give up something dear to us, negative events can cause us to cry for a night, but when we look up we see a beautiful butterfly trying to emerge from its cocoon.

Once I settled in at home and was moving toward dealing with my mother's cancer and the chaos my parents' household had erupted into, we were invited to attend a weekly cancer support meeting.

The leader, June Owen, had first uttered the above pearl of wisdom.

My mother attended in the beginning before going became too hard. My brother and his wife also attended some meetings in the beginning, but their own family demands with two small children made committing to attending challenging. My mother's parents tried to attend as well, but they were of a generation that couldn't sit down and talk about the dark stuff without tears flowing.

They were in their retirement years. My grandfather was 83, and my grandmother was 78. Their precious daughter, Peggy, was sick. It was a trial both were ill prepared for.

My mother was named after her two grandmothers. She never knew her paternal grandparents. Thomas and Margaret "Maggie"

Tuttle united in marriage at the turn of the century and had six children, my grandfather Roy being the oldest. He would later learn that his given name was Raymond, and Roy had developed somewhere along the line in his younger years.

Roy had already survived a major health crisis. In the fall of 1979, at 78 he had survived an incredible 12-hour operation to repair an aneurysm and to more or less reinstall his arterial plumbing.

My mother was ready to let him go during this crisis. She knew he had lived a good life. Yet Roy or "Bill," as his older friends and relatives called him, surprised everyone by not only surviving the challenge, but he reclaimed a sparky energy that the aneurysm had been robbing him of for years.

He loved being a grandpa to all of us, a role that suited him well. He especially loved small children, and they loved him. My brothers and sisters naturally gravitated to him, sitting on his lap, enjoying his old-time pranks and stories.

"Wanna know how a crow lights?" Grandpa Roy would challenge as he awaited the inevitable "how" from his intended victim.

"Like this," he would squeal in delight as he grabbed the leg of his intended victim and squeezed hard.

Now, Roy couldn't bear the thought of his daughter going through this ordeal. He quietly suffered through post-traumatic stress because his grandchildren were walking in his shoes when he was nine years old.

He never really talked about those years, but obviously they had taken a toll on his youth.

His mother had fallen victim to tuberculosis, leaving Roy and his six siblings to fend for themselves. The youngest, Francis, was taken in by another family and raised as their own.

Even though the story was incredible to believe, Francis was at a family dinner when she turned 50, and the true origin of her birth was revealed to her. A major rift was created within the family. The truth so shocked her that she was a Tuttle, not a Carroll, that she didn't speak to her biological sister, Mabel, for years.

So it was with the generation born in the early 1900s. Covering things up, sweeping them under the rug or putting your head in the sand was easier than plowing ahead with the truth.

Understanding of family history in regard to colon cancer would come later. My mother had an Uncle Mike who died of rectal cancer in 1968. Because of what my mother now had, her children would have to seek preventive care for this later on.

I led my siblings in obtaining preventative colonoscopies in the future in order to prevent the occurrence of colon cancer by the removal of polyps.

My grandmother, who had taught fifth grade during the turbulent 60s in the Kansas City suburb of Parkville, had a firm grasp on things out of books, but she couldn't totally embrace the reality of the illness that threatened her daughter's life.

I never understood the great pain my grandparents went through while their only child suffered at the hands of this relentless disease. For them, the world made no sense when someone so bright and vivacious as Peggy was felled by cancer.

My mother's illness defied logic in their eyes. Peggy didn't do the things that people who get cancer do. For them, Peggy wasn't the mature mother of nine who had made her own way in the world as a farmer's wife and a religious education leader.

No, for them, the little girl Peggy was the one who was sick.

The cancer support group offered open discussions, facts, figures, treatments and testimonies from people who had cancer. This forum wasn't suited to my grandparents, nor was it the right place for my brother and his wife. My father found value in it, but my mother struggled to talk about her situation.

"Does it make you angry?" June asked my mother one day.

My mother looked around the room, studying each of the faces sitting around the table. Maybe her reaction was because her parents were present, but she simply shrugged her shoulders and said, "No, I'm not angry."

I couldn't help focusing on the crucifix pinned to her blouse when she made that statement. I recalled the look on her face in the summer of the previous year when she begged for a kiss, something she never asked for.

No, if you were angry, you would never tell us. Your life was always about everyone else. You were even now worried about how this was affecting us. You were going to beat this thing. If you didn't accept it, then it couldn't take away your dreams of raising your children.

June introduced the Un Game to the participants gathered around the table. Intended to be an ice breaker, the game required each attendee to draw a card and to discuss or answer the statement or question posed on the card.

The Un Game card deck was pushed my way. I lifted the next card off the deck.

"What is your worst fear?"

I gazed across the room into my mother's eyes.

The echo of my voice from yesteryear called me into focus. "It's not easy being creative."

Then as now, my mother said not a word. She was smiling at me. She knew what I was going to say.

"My biggest fear is that I will lose my mother to cancer."

Everyone around the table gazed at me in wonder when I expressed the unthinkable thought out loud. My mother simply nodded.

An advocate for colon cancer and cancer support had just been born. I would be the person who stuck with the group throughout and kept them updated on Mom's progress and her setbacks.

I went from being a quiet observer to being an active, passionate caregiver. Within my calling this year were also responsibilities that weren't mine to carry.

Like my cousin, Steve, I would accept more than was my share, but I had just taken the first step toward learning a truth about the process.

This will make you stronger still.

The community rallies

The result of seeking out a second opinion with Dr. Munson, an oncologist at St. Luke's Regional Medical Center in Kansas City, was the determination of an aggressive treatment plan that included five weeks of daily radiation treatments.

Mom refused to stay in Kansas City, choosing instead to be at home daily with her kids. That left a dilemma for my father who needed to keep operating the farm at a time when planting season would be in full swing.

It was decided. I would serve as the chauffeur, driving two

hours each way for the treatments, which would take less than an hour. Mom's reward was seeing a huge ceiling poster of Tom Selleck of *Magnum PI* fame that kept her focus off the cancerous tumor the radiation was working to shrink.

Many people were amazed by this decision, but I never questioned it.

Living in my mother's home, I had as the ultimate goal her comfort and her preferences. It was now May of 1984, nearly five months after her diagnosis.

In April, we celebrated the glory of my parents' 30 years together in Parnell. The smile on her face in the 30th anniversary pictures belied the truth. The tumor was growing, making sitting more difficult, and if something wasn't done, she would die an excruciatingly painful death as a result of that tumor.

We were all still in the "we will find a cure" mindset. Even though the possibility existed that this cancer would eventually take her life, we were in necessary denial. Life could only be taken day by day. Tomorrow would have to take care of itself.

Those outside our family were shaken by the prospects of this cancer.

Which is why the 30th anniversary celebration was birthed as a miracle from God. It wasn't just a gathering of family and friends, it was a testament that Peggy was not allowing this cancer to negatively rule her life.

The radiance that shone from her spirit that day, as reflected in the photos, didn't betray the existence of the decaying disease she was now fighting with every ounce of faith and strength.

She had to accept many things that were hard to accept. She had to discontinue going to church because the pews were too hard to sit on. She had to take to lying down in bed and resting, keeping by her side the portable phone that was her connection to the outside world.

The community rallied with cards, letters and well-wishes in the beginning, the community of sisters in my father's family rallied to clean the house from head to toe, the community of the church rallied to cook daily meals delivered by a church family each night and the community of the cancer support group kept me afloat by allowing me to talk about this beast and to help others understand ways of coping.

I was able to land a part-time, weekend job three days a week at a Christian radio station in Shenandoah, Iowa, just 50 miles northwest of the farm. That just added to the restrictions on my social life, which at this juncture was not a priority.

A benefit was put on for the family, the proceeds of which my father turned over to me. I was both honored and humbled by his act. He expressed his appreciation for my putting my life on hold and helping him with the task of running the household through this trial.

The gift and the job came in a timely manner as I needed new tires, and I went into the bank to rewrite the six-month note into a loan with manageable monthly payments.

Life was far from perfect in the summer of 1984, but it was good.

The call to service

God had given me a gift of counseling and understanding others. It existed during my teen years when I would defend those who were less blessed than I. I was always for the underdog and I knew somehow instinctively that a person's life experiences affected actions of today.

My gift developed after I left home for the military, when my peers would come to me with problems and ask for help in solving them.

Likewise, I became a sounding board for my father. All the walls between parent and child had come down. Nineteen-eighty-four was unique in that it bonded us like no other time in our lives.

In 1984, I felt activity in my sense of calling. In 1980, a priest had hinted my life's experiences and my broken engagement could be indicating a call to the priesthood, which I rejected out of hand.

Now, Father Regis also was hinting strongly at the possibility.
Lean not on your own understanding.

Would I have been able to come home and help out if I were married and established in my career? Would I be as footloose and fancy free to make decisions as I had?

The hard facts of that situation answered no. A further examination of those facts said to me that when I uttered a prayer in my small house in Hobbs, New Mexico, God answered, though not in the way I would have expected.

Maybe the truth was, I didn't utter the prayer under my own volition. Maybe the Holy Spirit had led me to pray those words, preparing me for what was to come.

I had no doubt blocks existed in the way of me launching my career and getting on with my life, and also didn't I come back to God at the age of 21 after a mind-altering experience?

Why then, did this twisted road always seem to lead to detours?

In 1984, I hadn't yet come to understand the precepts of what I call the process. However, the command to "lean not on your own understanding" is as powerful as "all things work together for the good."

God was somehow lifting me up, giving me the strength to move forward toward the goal, whatever that goal was.

I was also the oldest, so the responsibility naturally fell on my shoulders. And I took on this responsibility, foisted on me by my parents. Maybe I had failed to fully develop as the person I should have been. Maybe I was co-dependent.

I wanted to believe our family was immune to tragedy. My faith had been fragile many times throughout my life, but in 1984 I was asked a very serious question about my future. Without Christ, I could do nothing.

I had to consider the possibility that God might be calling me to the priesthood.

I would struggle with this question in 1984 and put it to rest once and for all. Even though I tried to do everything I could do to change the circumstance in the first 30 years of my life, I was called to the single life.

I would learn that bachelorhood was just as valuable a call as any other. God had deeper purposes in mind when Regina and I gave up on our broken relationship.

Now, I was the one available to put forth the time and effort to drive my mother daily to her radiation treatments in Kansas City.

I always knew the truth. My mother had already beaten two months. Now, unless we had a parting of the Red Sea, she wouldn't live to see Christmas. It was a thought that wouldn't do us any good.

So we simply ignored it.

13 - CRISIS OF FAITH

The radiation treatments were a success, not in the way my mother would have hoped, but the tumor did shrink, and the pain subsided. She became somewhat more active, still running the household from her bed, but able to enjoy more activity.

"I don't know what it means, but I itch like crazy," my mother commented toward the end of the treatments.

"Maybe that's a good sign," I said hopefully.

"I'm just going to believe it is," she said and then dropped the subject.

Well-wishers would call and fuss and proclaim that they didn't want to bother her, but I would insist that they talk to her, knowing she needed that fuel to remain connected to the outside world.

I lived the summer months fully. My radio job kept my mind off the detour taking place in my life and kept some money trickling in. I was still needed in a capacity to keep the household running smoothly, and my two sisters, Linda and Nancy, were forced to lose some of their childhood as they stepped up to meet the demands of the household chores.

There came the day that Mom decided to make a silent declaration. She donned a shirt and shorts and sat in her chair in the living room. I came downstairs and stopped dead in my tracks as I gazed at her, speechless.

Again, she said not a word, but the frail woman in front of me was a ghost of a person. How had she hidden the fact that she had lost so much weight? It had become so easy not to talk about the elephant in the room—but that was a necessary ingredient in our recipe for survival.

Again in August, family and friends gathered for her 51st birthday. We had a celebration at the farm for my father's family and a celebration at the park for relatives on my mother's side.

The happy times were almost over. In mid-September, Mom got sick, and we had to transport her to St. Luke's Hospital in Kansas City to determine a course of action. She was released twice and taken in three times.

On the third trip, Dr. Munson came to my father and me.

"Nothing more can be done," he said gravely. "I recommend she be transferred to your local hospital. I'm sorry."

We both nodded, yet we were numb with shock. I understood what he was saying, but I refused to own it. Looking back, I saw that the depth of my denial was fathoms deep. Yet, when the doctor spoke about her returning to the Maryville hospital, I knew the truth.

Still, my faith, which in 1980 would have espoused that if I prayed for it, I would receive it, was waffling in the wind. I was failing to believe that anything positive could happen. I didn't dare believe it, because if I did and nothing good happened, then maybe my God wasn't real.

On this platform, God dealt with me in very real and defining ways in 1984. That's where I had missed the boat.

Father Regis had declared "it was not over" at a funeral, yet I was on a collision course with this priest, who would demand that I declare the battle over.

I heard lots of talk about God's will in 1984, but how could this be God's will?

I as of yet didn't know the conversations my mother and father had in the barren years, the years when she, as an only child, desired more children.

"My prayers will never be answered," she said as she gently laid her head on his chest.

"My dear," my father whispered, "you know that if God wants you to have more children, he will hear your prayers."

Who had the most faith? My father who was raised a Catholic

and always believed in God, or my mother who struggled with the questions posed by being raised in a household split by the religious matters in life?

I imagined my grandmother's struggles with the same issues.

"I did everything you wanted me to do, but still you chose that my boys should succumb to death. You have only given me a daughter. Why?"

The silence must have been deafening to her. Maybe it was the reason she had such difficulty stepping across the line into an active faith in the church. She attended church faithfully with Grandpa Roy, but was never baptized herself.

The day did come when she stepped across that line due to my mother's persistence.

Naomi Tuttle, at the age of 78, was baptized into the Catholic faith during an Easter Vigil service.

And when she was baptized, God responded with a lightning bolt crackling outside the small Parnell parish at the exact moment she declared her faith to the congregation.

That was all my mother needed to know that God had answered her prayers, and she smiled at my father.

Where was that lightning bolt today?

Initially, the family doctor had failed to sit us all down to explain the harsh realities of our journey ahead. Instead, he had taken on a sense of responsibility himself and decided to play God by refusing to refer my mother to a specialist who might at least be able to add to the time she had left.

When he had discovered the spread of the disease to the liver, he shouldn't have given in to defeat. That was his human error. He underestimated my mother's resolve; he took it upon himself to decide what was best.

The cancer wasn't going to go away on its own. My mother had an entire summer ahead of her, and she lived it to the fullest following the radiation treatments that didn't cure her, but gave her the miracle of extra time with her family to say goodbye.

She didn't succumb to the negativity of a lack of faith, but I had. My own crisis of faith was so focused on how everything affected me that I failed to see that, yes, in all sadness there is joy, in all joy there is sadness.

I was able to follow my mother's lead in dealing with the

disease, but I wasn't able to embrace the truth of what the disease was trying to teach me, nor were many other people able to grasp the miracle in their midst.

Mom's courage in the face of the inevitability helped keep the denial alive. Those who didn't live in the farmhouse had a much more realistic portrait of the physical reality, but they couldn't see the spiritual reality: my mother's faith that defied all understanding.

My mother was admitted to St. Francis Hospital. My father, his mother, my mother's parents, my brother and his wife and I kept a vigil at the hospital. Grandpa George couldn't tolerate hospitals and only visited my mother once, but he made the pilgrimage, to his credit.

Many well-wishers stopped by, including a large number I'd never seen before in my life, a testament to my mother's far-reaching influence in Nodaway County and beyond.

Ministers and priests would visit my mother, and a disturbing trend began to emerge. The priests seemed to be focused on the negativity. Prayers of death would close in on me, and one day I emerged out of the room in a fit of anger.

"What's wrong?" my father asked, concerned.

"They just whisper as if she can't hear, and all they can talk about is dying."

My father believed if a miracle was going to happen, it would. I believed each day was one more miracle. My mother kept talking about going home while one minister prayed over her and explained that she'd be ready to go to whichever home that the Lord called her to.

My mother would smile and nod her head yes.

One day, I was in the room alone with her when she looked over her left shoulder and up behind her.

"Hear that?" she said.

"What?" I asked, looking at the wall, puzzled by her actions. "Hear what?"

"Water."

A smile crept across her face as she relaxed and lay her head back in the bed.

Instantly an image of a waterfall formed in my mind. Something spiritual was happening. I didn't know what—only my mother knew—but I felt a peaceful knowing that my mother had just experienced a heavenly vision.

I had never seen the stages of death before. We were ill-prepared for going through this process. My father and I stood together, hopeful for the future, but as I found out many years later, Mom's talk of home had nothing to do with heaven.

She wanted to go home to be with her kids. They were her life, after all. She had prayed to God to be blessed with more children. God had answered. Why couldn't she go home?

Facing reality

In the second week at Maryville, Father Regis, who had so inspired me at Orville Durbin's funeral and had moved my faith beyond any obstacles or mountains in front of me, knocked me off that pedestal.

I met him in the hallway of the main entrance as he was leaving.

"I'm so sorry for you and your family," he offered. The somberness in his tone was different. His facial expressions were etched in stone, and his voice was very grave. "Marvin, you must hand her over to the Lord now. You must let her go."

I stared at the man in black, dumbfounded. All that these men of my parents' faith could talk about was death; they couldn't wait until the dirt was thrown on my mother's gravesite.

"We still have hope," I responded.

"There is no place for false hope." The priest's eyes conveyed pity at my optimism.

"You don't understand." I turned my back on the priest who had become my mother's spiritual mentor through this journey. He was making my own journey difficult. He was challenging my own core beliefs about God and Jesus Christ.

When I got home, I called my sister-in-law and felt the frustration and anger at his request rising in me.

"He actually said that?"

"Yes," I said, still reeling from the pain of the suggestion.

She was shocked but didn't know how to comfort me.

I had to go to work at the radio station that night. I was arriving at my first stage of anger. The stage my mother said she never went through, but that was months before. This was now.

During my shift, at 2 a.m. in the morning, as a Christian radio show went out over the airways, I picked up the phone and irrationally called my Aunt Dee out of bed.

I expressed the anger I felt, and then her voice pushed through the phone lines with words I couldn't readily accept.

"Marvin, this is now up to Peggy. She has fought the tough fight. It's up to her now. Father Regis is human too. He just wants to soften the blow. You know, if your mom could beat this, she would. Maybe God wants you to know what's coming. You can have hope, but you also have to face reality."

After I apologized for calling at such an insane hour and hung up, the pit of my depression gobbled me up. I had been the strong one, the rock for my father, the martyr for my mother. I had nowhere to take my fears to now. My aunt had given me what I needed to walk across the tightrope of acceptance.

My mother was dying. I always knew it, but if I gave up on hope, what was left? How did I face her tomorrow or the next day? Hope was her lifeline for the quality of life she was living.

The riverbank experience

Many people told us about the prayers that were going up for us. After my 2 a.m. call with my aunt, she came to Maryville for a day and we hung out, drifting in conversation and seeking out wise counselors.

One such counselor was another aunt who had a word from God to me that stunned and shocked me.

"Do the kids know your mother is dying?" Aunt Marilyn asked, relaying a similar situation in her family in which the transition and preparation for saying goodbye was difficult.

I stared at her dumbfounded. "No, I guess not. We don't really talk about it. They know things are serious, but we've never discussed that possibility."

I didn't realize it at the time, but Father Regis had plowed the ground to allow me to deliver the message to my younger siblings. I knew my father wasn't up to the task.

I made plans to talk to the kids when I got home and then take them to see our mother. Once I made that decision, God provided me with the strength to carry out the task.

I told them in groups. I called in the three older boys, David,

Dean and Norbert. I eased into it, but even though they met the news with some resistance, they took it in stride and could now support each other because now they knew the truth.

"We still hope things work out, but I have to let you know that Mama may not make it. She's very sick and she could die."

The words sort of stuck in my throat as I told my two sisters, Linda and Nancy. The response from Nancy tore at my heart. She giggled and she couldn't stop.

"It's okay," I soothed her. "It's a nervous giggle. This is big news to take."

"But I can't stop laughing."

"It's okay. You're nervous because you're scared. It's okay to be scared. So am I."

The hardest pair to tell was Roland and Karl. Only in the second grade, Karl had been the extrovert growing up in this family of nine, the baby. Roland was the quiet one and had a special attachment to my mother.

As I struggled to tell them, I was amazed at the strength they displayed in listening. Neither one really knew how to respond. I hugged them both.

When they left the room, I took a deep breath. I was grateful to Marilyn and Dee for helping me realize this had to be done.

While we were driving to Maryville to see our mother, Nancy's voice came from the backseat.

"What is cancer?"

I eyed her in the rearview mirror and attempted to come up with a reasonable answer for an 11-year-old. I realized that Dad and I had managed to support each other, but somehow in the spirit of our mutual support and holding each other up, we had fallen behind on keeping the kids in the loop.

The prayers everyone had been praying weren't healing my mother, but they were guiding me along the path of her last days. They gave me the courage and the strength to be there for my family in order to prepare them for what was coming.

14 - THE AFTERMATH

My mother was failing fast. She was no longer eating, but she was always cheered by the visitors who entered her room: people I had never met, women who remembered the little girl in blond curls, friendships that had lingered in memory as new experiences were lived and savored.

In the backdrop of the past few months there had been a special friend, a "sister" so to speak. Teddy Runde and my mother were practically joined at the hip through their common involvement in the Kansas City Diocese catechism program.

The friendship was unique as Teddy was so much the opposite of my mother; yet the bond that they had couldn't be denied. My father allowed a moment or two of jealousy to erupt during those last days, and as a spectator I observed the conflict.

It was part of the stress of our emotional storm.

As Karl was the son who was the outgoing one, and Roland entered school and the older siblings provided babysitting services, Mom's last few years had been lived outside the home when she became part of a wider community.

God had called her to a larger role in the church, and she had answered that call with enthusiasm. My father was less than enthused about it, often pointing out that she could learn to say no a little more often.

He had to adjust to her new role as a community person, and

as such she was also in direct competition with her mother. An only child, the full brunt of "back seat parenting" was borne by my mother who understood the complexities of childhood and sibling rivalry. She had found a plethora of brothers and sisters in my father's family and it filled a need in her life to be part of a larger family unit.

"You know we're all praying for Peggy." Teddy outstretched her hand and embraced me when I entered the room. "I couldn't have asked for a better sister."

I smiled at my mother and realized for the first time what the 'sister' bond meant to Teddy and my mother.

They were sisters in Christ.

Linda's 13th birthday arrived on Tuesday, October 16th. It was not to be celebrated in the shadows. We brought her birthday to my mother's hospital room.

My mother had anticipated the event and seemed to enjoy light banter and laughter even though she couldn't enjoy any of the birthday cake.

The next day I walked into her room, basking in the glow of the revelry of the day before.

My mother was radiant and sitting up fully in her bed.

"When are we celebrating Linda's birthday?" she asked cheerfully and with anticipation. "I'm feeling rather chipper today."

I stopped short and searched for the right thing to say, yet failed miserably. "But," I stammered, "Linda's birthday was yesterday. Don't you remember?"

I just as well have punched my mother in the stomach. She folded into emotion and sank into the bed. She had lost a day, a day she couldn't remember, a day that held one of her fondest wishes in what had become a tiring battle.

My own optimism sank as I realized my mother was fast slipping away. I sat with her, trying to ignore the elephant in the room and encouraging her to make the most of whatever she had left to live in this life.

On Thursday evening, I answered the phone by her bedside.

"Hello," I responded cheerfully.

"Yeah, Marvin, we're getting ready to come over," David said.

"Sure thing, David," I said.

But my mother resolutely signaled to me that my brother's request shouldn't be granted when she shook her head and closed her eyes. Dad held her hand and didn't know how to help his wife at this moment.

"Ah, David, maybe you better not come over tonight. Mom's not feeling up to it right now, maybe tomorrow." I had no idea how cruel my words must have sounded. This would be the last time any of my brothers and sisters would have been able to see my mother, and I allowed her to call the shots.

It was the first real sign that my mother was resigning herself to the inevitable.

Years later, I would realize my mistake and also recognize the fragile balance between granting a loved one's wishes and doing what was best in the long run. David never knew until years later that it was my mother who had nixed the visit.

On the afternoon of October 19th, 1984, I called the radio station to inform them I wouldn't be in all three days of my work shifts. The end was near. I sensed as much. For three weeks I had been in denial of what was happening, holding it away from myself, refusing to take it in, but I knew now that the inevitable was on its way.

"There was a second death on the floor last night," my father said somberly. "Things do happen in threes. I've seen it before."

I nodded in agreement as I stood by his side in this hour of need.

My father somehow talked my grandparents into going home and resting. The bedside vigil was becoming a burden on them.

My grandmother was also experiencing a post traumatic stress event of her own. She blamed herself for not being by her father's bedside when he died. She didn't want the same fate to occur now with her daughter; however, her own weariness signaled to her that going home was probably best.

Aunt Donna had gone to the farmhouse after school, helped fix supper for my younger siblings and then drove the four youngest to Vincent and Joan's house. The three boys went to stay with Grandma and Grandpa Tuttle.

I was also feeling the toll of the vigil, and I also opted to leave later that night as Mom's breathing became more labored. The hospital staff was gently preparing us as they indicated the end was near.

Staying at the hospital were my father, my brother and Grandma Gertrude who prayed her rosary softly at Mom's bedside.

I fell asleep on the couch in my brother's living room.

Suddenly, in my dream state, my consciousness was filled with the burst of a bright light as it engulfed everything. A sense of calm and peace accompanied the dream of no words or visions, except light.

I opened my eyes, and my brother stood before me in the doorway. Before he even spoke, I knew.

My mother had died.

Dreams in the night

The women of the small St. Joseph parish were in constant prayer for their sister Peggy who had been besieged by this beast called cancer.

They had worked side by side with her at many a parish bazaar and laughed and shared many joys and tragedies at social events. Her presence at the church was sorely missed.

The church community had been especially hard hit that tragedy had been so cruel since their leader, Father Regis, had come to this parish.

Not only did the death of Orville Durbin hit the community hard, but David Runde, another lay church leader, had been killed in a car accident.

Now, Peggy Wilmes was dying of cancer at St. Francis Hospital.

Pat Auffert ended her day quietly after cleaning up the supper dishes and watching some television with her husband.

She remembered Peggy in her nighttime prayers as she dozed off and fell into a peaceful slumber.

The phone rang, and she got up to answer it.

"Hello," she said, rubbing her tired eyes.

"Pat, I just wanted to call you and thank you for all you and the church have done for me and my family. I love you."

"Love you too."

Startled, Pat sat up in bed and stared into the darkness.

It took her a moment, but once she got her bearings, she

realized she had dreamed the conversation.

She cried and feared the worst. As she lay back down, she was going to make sure she passed the message on.

Safely Home

The next 12 hours were a blur. My brother, father and I got into the car and headed to Ravenwood to deliver the news to my grandparents.

David, Dean and Norbert were staying there as well. In order to provide more support for my grandparents, we stopped by to notify my grandmother's brother, Victor, and his wife, Thelma.

"Oh my God," my grandfather wailed. "If only she had seen her kids graduate. Why couldn't she see her kids graduate."

I instinctively rubbed my grandfather's back as his frame shook with emotion, and my grandmother folded into a sea of grief that swept us all away.

"My little girl," Naomi said as her brother, Victor, comforted her.

I was in a state of shock. We discussed funeral plans and other details. Dad wanted to have the funeral as soon as possible. Without our giving it any thought, Mom's death was about to infringe on my brother Dean's 16th birthday, a detail lost on us until the day arrived.

That's how rapidly the aftermath of her death took us by storm, and in some ways, it kept my Dad and me moving by keeping us busy with the details. After we informed the rest of my siblings, Dad and my grandparents went and made the arrangements on Saturday. I set about making sure everyone was informed.

Leo and Marjorie. I made a sudden mental note to call two of Mom and Dad's best friends at the time they were dating, who'd popped into my head.

"Hello," Marjorie answered the phone.

"Hi, Marjorie, this is Marvin, I just wanted you to know that Mom died last night."

"Oh I'm so sorry," she exclaimed. "Thank you for calling and letting us know."

The family rosary was 24 hours after her death, an incredibly short time by any standards. It probably revealed a much-too-rushed affair, but for Dad, it was important to show acceptance, or was it a hurry to finalize the event? It didn't matter. We were both robots in the process at the moment.

As family filed past my siblings offering their condolences, Karl allowed all of his emotion out while Roland sat stoically with his hands in his lap. Everyone was grieving differently and although Karl's meltdown was hard to watch while Mom's cousin Ellen Remick hugged him with massive force, emotion was something I was glad Karl could experience fully.

The parish rosary was on Sunday night.

Leo Dierks walked by me and suddenly embraced me with that same bear hug energy and tearfully whispered in my ear, "Thank you for all you did for her."

For the first time I came to realize just what 1984 had meant to me. Everything in my life had been suspended and the reality of my loss washed over me. I hadn't really owned my life—I had given it. I had never had a question as to what I should do in the matter. I just did it.

I tucked Leo's words and Pat's report of her dream in my pocket for future reference when I felt lost in the sea of grief I would cope with.

Suddenly, while I numbly shook hands and mumbled thanks to the many people who were sorry for our loss, I was transported back in time to the prayer I had uttered in my small living room in Hobbs, New Mexico.

Tears welled in my eyes as I realized yesterday was gone and tomorrow was yet to be revealed. Grief was wrapping its cold, wet fingers around my throat and I didn't know who I was at the moment except the role of advocate, caregiver and my father's deepest confidant.

The church was packed on the day of the funeral. Seeing my mother's slight body lying in the casket, I was taken by her frailty. She was sleeping so peacefully, I felt a sense of joy that her suffering was over, which seemed oddly placed.

The music chosen stirred my soul beyond compare. *Amazing Grace* and *How Great Thou Art* made the earth tremble beneath my feet as I sang with a confidence and strength befitting an opera singer.

My father's voice was the loudest, and my spirit was buoyed

by the knowledge that my mother was safely home.

"Alfred." Father Regis touched my father's shoulder at the conclusion of the service and thrust an object in his hand. The priest couldn't hold back the tears.

We walked out of the church and gathered on the front lawn while the pallbearers loaded Mom's casket into the hearse. My father approached me, put his hand out and opened it.

When I saw what lay in his hand, tears cascaded down my cheeks, and we embraced in a moment that never will repeat itself in our lives. We had come to the pinnacle of the mountaintop experience in our father and son relationship. Words didn't have to be spoken.

In his hand, gleaming in the sun was another crucifix like the one my mother wore through her illness, the one my father had made sure was pinned to her dress the day of her burial. Father Regis had given my father the ornament that spoke volumes about the journey we had been on and the journey we were setting out on.

My mother's cancer had been her cross to bear. Now, it was our turn to pick up our cross and move forward without her grace to guide us or lead us.

Safely Home by Unknown

I am home in Heaven, dear ones; Oh, so happy and so bright
There is perfect joy and beauty; In this everlasting light.
All the pain and grief is over: Every restless tossing passed;
I am now at peace forever, Safely home in Heaven at last.

Did you wonder I so calmly Trod the valley of the shade?
Oh! but Jesus' arm to lean on, Could I have one doubt or dread?
Then you must not grieve so sorely, For I love you dearly still;
Try to look beyond earth's shadows, Pray to trust our Father's Will.

There is work still waiting for you, So you must not idly stand;
Do it now, while life remaineth– You shall rest in Jesus' land.
When that work is all completed, He will gently call you Home;
Oh, the rapture of that meeting, Oh, the joy to see you come!

The final goodbye

Emotions only flowed more freely at the cemetery where everyone gathered around the gravesite and whispered their final goodbyes. Once Mom's casket was lowered into the ground, the finality of it bore down on our family like a huge anvil.

As people passed by and offered handshakes, tear-filled hugs and condolences, an elderly woman in the parish by the name of Marie Waske walked up to me. I only knew her as a member of the parish, an acquaintance, nothing more.

"If you think this is bad, just wait." Her embrace caught me off guard, and she squeezed hard. Her words swirled in my mind, and I thanked her for her concern.

What are you talking about? If you think this is bad, just wait. What kind of thing is that to say to someone in grief?

I didn't know it at the time, but of the entire day, that sentence would stand out and weather the test of time. Marie Waske was giving me a word from God. He was wanting me to remember it, but not as a testament to doom and gloom and hopelessness.

Rather, it was a testament to "the process."

Father Regis had proclaimed in his sermon that "he will do greater things." In 1980, in the aftermath of my broken engagement with Regina, I had learned that "all things work together for the good."

Standing at the Parnell Cemetery listening to those words of hopelessness, I was reminded of Father Regis' demand that I let Mom go. Today was that day, but he'd wanted it done a week prior.

I wasn't ready then, nor should I have been.

If you think this is bad, just wait.

Was she right? Maybe.

However, I had no idea that I was beginning a journey of discovery to learn what faith was really about.

Happiness is found along the way, not at the end of the road.

What is happiness? What is the secret to life that everybody is searching for? Mom had found it. I knew that. In her short life, she'd managed to affect her world in a huge way. She never gave up until the very end as she fought her cancer battle. She took a two-month prognosis and turned it into a nine-month celebration of life. She took the time to smell the roses and to properly say goodbye without giving in to negativity.

In all joy, there is sadness; in all sadness, there is joy.

A year before, I wouldn't have understood this in its entirety, but after I shook off Marie Waske's words, I experienced the joy, as my heart was glad that Mom was no longer suffering and had gone home to her Lord.

I knew without a doubt that it was her spirit which had filled my consciousness with that bright light in my dream at the point of her death.

I smiled when I realized God had granted my mother and me a final goodbye.

15 - ASHES TO ASHES, DUST TO DUST

Days turned into weeks while the drudgery of life after Mom's death settled in like the coming of the winter months.

The month of November was a lonely one. People had stopped calling and stopped checking in on us. Things were changing for my brothers and sisters at school, too, since they'd been coddled during Mom's illness but were now expected to step up and get over it, as if you could just remove a person from your household and go on as though nothing had ever happened.

Karl was approaching his eighth birthday, and he assumed the negative belief that his birthday party in the second grade wouldn't happen this year because Mom wasn't there to pull it off.

"My birthday is next week," my brother interrupted my father and me, discussing the latest world issues.

"Yes and you'll be eight. That's exciting."

Karl stood solid in front of me and never flinched. He waited patiently for me to pick up on his body language.

"What's on your mind?" I asked.

"I don't have anyone to take birthday treats to my class."

I was amazed at his calm demeanor while he laid out his dilemma for us to finally realize what was close to the end of the world for him.

"Oh, well, you can have a birthday party at school." I laughed nervously when I suddenly realized I would be the one to undertake this task for the family. I assured Karl that his birthday would be celebrated, and I stepped in as the substitute.

I was once again in the second grade room where Mrs. Lewis had reprimanded me for teaching her class and Tom Birkenholz had shunned me for being just slightly taller than he.

Karl's eyes revealed the treasure in the moment. For now at least, life was going to be somewhat normal for him.

As the Christmas season approached, the icy hands of depression began to grip our household, and it had brought down my mother's parents as well.

My father and I had to visit them on a cold November day as we felt they were shutting us out. It was not just our imagination either.

Grief was playing tricks on their minds and depression was moving in. Grandpa Roy's sister Mabel helped keep them socially afloat and offered the supports she could, but she also needed our help as she secretly feared for the couple's safety.

I sensed the impending exercise was going to be painful, but in the aftermath of Grandpa Roy's explosion, I was grateful we had opened the discussion.

"Yeah, I've thought about what could happen with the car running in the basement with the garage door shut," his face was flush with anger as I secretly wished I had been wrong about what his depression could turn into.

"Peggy was our daughter, damn it and I'll be damned if I am going to have you come in here and act like this isn't something that affects us."

The confrontation had gotten out of hand and I was never so grateful that Mabel had been present to referee the dispute. Everyone was in tears and I felt miserable at having entered into the discussion.

Mabel took me aside in the living room after calmer heads prevailed and my father and grandfather returned to light banter.

"Marvin, I do believe this did your grandfather a world of good. He was blazing mad and I've been watching him mope around the house as if his life is over," she said. "He'll be all right, I'll watch after them. He needed to get the fire in his belly. Don't fret none."

"Thanks," I said somewhat taken aback by Mabel's optimistic tone, but time proved that Grandpa Roy's anger had been just the antidote to cure what ailed him.

Surprisingly, he would live another 12 years and prove just how "tough as nails" he was.

Anger was yet to descend on my soul, but I would get my turn soon enough.

My mother's social club invited my family to share their Christmas meeting with them. I was beginning to feel unsure of where I belonged in the world. As of yet, searching for a job hadn't been a top priority. I was busy maintaining an atmosphere of transition for the family without the security of my mother's voice coming from the bedroom.

At times, the silence was deafening.

Aunt Dee visited with Joan and me to discuss going through my mother's clothes, the task of removing her presence. We decided to do this while my father was busy in the field so as to reduce his pain.

"Why is everyone walking on eggshells around me?" He demanded an answer from me after he discovered we'd removed her clothes from the closet without him being present.

Everything about this new experience was similar in that the reactions of those in the house were different than what the rest of us anticipated. Each family member wanted to protect the other. The thing was, we had no way to insulate anyone from the loss experienced.

It affected each person differently.

For me, the issue of the priesthood arose front and center. Father Regis was targeting his sermons right in my direction, and my antennae were acutely tuned into his reasoning.

Maybe Father Helfry, the priest who had helped me face the inevitability of the end of my relationship with Regina, had been right. Maybe God was calling me to the priesthood.

"That is a big, big decision," Aunt Dee said as we sat around the table, delaying the task of removing my mother's clothes from the closet because it was too final an act. "You've just been through a major trauma. You need to really pray about that."

I knew she was right, again. She often was. Talking to her always put my head on straight. God had used her many times in my life to guide me along the rocky path.

She'd undergone a lot of pain in her life as well. I was as of yet unaware that she had given birth to a baby girl while still in high school. Plus, I was as yet unable to talk to her about her nephew, Steve's, death.

These were all conversations for a decade down the road.

I took my aunt's advice under advisement and brought the suggestion of the call to God. I placed it firmly in His hands.

Within days, I got the answer.

Door of opportunity

In 1982, prior to my employment with KHOB in Hobbs, New Mexico, my mother and father offered their support in driving me through a large regional area to drop off resumes and aircheck tapes at local radio stations.

The trip took us as far away as Trenton, Missouri; Red Oak, Iowa; and Atchison, Kansas. It gave us time to share in laughter and adult banter, while allowing me to feel that something was being done in launching my career.

All efforts failed, or at the very least, lay dormant. Our trek counted as a valiant effort, one long ago forgotten when I traveled to two other radio jobs and into the trials of 1984.

But on a brisk December day, the telephone in the kitchen rang. I picked it up, expecting to hear from a friend or relative who wanted to see how we were doing.

"This is Harold Shoeppner of KARE radio in Atchison, Kansas. I remember you visited our radio station a while back and dropped off an aircheck and resume. I wondered if you were still interested in a position with our station."

I was stunned. I recalled crossing the Missouri River south and west of St. Joseph, Missouri. The station was a mere hour-and-a-half away from our home. My experience at KYFR and KHOB gave me a shot at being able to land this position. Once again, I wasn't as concerned with economics as landing a fulltime position and moving up on the career ladder.

I scheduled the interview, and that evening I would eat a Christmas dinner at the club-hosted event with my family and then planned to leave early to head to Shenendoah for my Friday night shift.

I felt as if the phone call had allowed me to turn an important personal corner in my own trial of life. Maybe joy was about to come in the morning. Maybe I could begin to believe in my personal dawn.

The fiery furnace

My heart was light when I drove home after my overnight shift. I was singing to the radio and tapping the steering wheel with the beat as I crested the hill above the farmhouse, and my heart temporarily skipped a beat.

My father's pickup was backed up to the front porch. The position of the vehicle was all wrong. What possible reason could Dad have had to back it into the yard? I felt my breath being sucked away, and I had a sixth sense in my gut that something was terribly off track.

As I walked up to the front porch, my Dad greeted me with a big grin plastered across his face. Again, I had the memory of the young man who swiped his brow with his hat raised in my childhood, who was about to make an earth-shattering statement. I waited with anticipation for his proclamation.

"We had an interesting night. When we got home, we discovered the kitchen was on fire." He turned and strode into the house, and I silently followed.

What greeted me was a smoke-stained house and the stench of a fire-ravaged home. Dad went on to explain that the house suffered mainly smoke damage, which had permeated every nook and cranny of the living space.

Dad had asked the older boys to go to the neighbor's house and call 911. He asked the younger kids to stay put while he entered the house. The floor of the kitchen was engulfed in flames.

He realized he couldn't fight the fire himself, and he quickly exited the house so as not to be overcome by the smoke nor to create a further fanning of the flames because the enclosed space was containing the fire somewhat.

After area fire departments responded to put out the blaze, an investigation of the aftermath revealed the culprit. Even though the coffee pot was turned off, the plug had been defective and the fire started there.

I surveyed the damage with my father, and my eyes fell upon

the barometer that was now a melted, molten mess. Nothing was left of it.

I was amazed, however, that just above it was my mother and father's 30th anniversary picture. It was unscathed, untouched. It had nary a singe.

She's watching over us.

Nothing else could explain why the fire hadn't become an inferno and burned up everything inside. Nothing else could explain why no one was home at the time, and everyone had been safe from danger.

I would have little sleep between radio shifts that day since all I could do was join my father in laughter.

"So what else can there be?"

This was number three in a line of mishaps in the fall of 1984. My sister Linda had just weeks ago come down with a virus, recording a 104-degree temperature. My dad was quiet as he rushed her to the emergency room in Maryville.

She was given antibiotics and got over her illness, but being oversensitive to our loss, we secretly had feared the worst.

Now, my father laughed. "There's nothing to do but dig in and put things back together. We were fortunate the whole house didn't go up in flames. Most of the smoke damage is upstairs. Everything is covered in smoke."

Once again, my father's family rallied around him. We saved what we could and hauled furniture and other smoke-damaged items out to the machine shed. We had to throw away lots of stuff, including my long-standing album collection, which included the Commodore album and the swan song of my relationship with Regina.

I felt as if the past had also gone up in smoke, and painful memories were both resurrected and simultaneously erased.

Clothes were laundered, walls were scrubbed and a contractor was brought in to clean the carpets and walls and to restore the house to a sensible condition. But the contractor clearly wasn't going to deliver on what he promised, so my father had to send him on his way and a massive scrub-down family party was scheduled with Raymond, Joe, Vincent and their spouses coming out to help.

My father went on a shopping spree following' filing the

insurance claim. He was relieved that the insurance covered most of the damage.

The fire split up the family once again. Linda, Nancy, Roland and Karl stayed with my grandparents in Ravenwood and David, Dean and Norbert stayed at Joe and Donna's, our uncle and aunt who lived nearby. Dad and I also stayed there.

A reporter from the *St. Joseph Gazette* got wind of the story, and we became the center of attention as the subjects of a Christmas tragedy feature with a tinge of the miraculous. I testified to the value of our faith in dealing with the dual tragedies of my mother's death and the fire.

Harold Schoeppner apparently read the story as well prior to my interview, something I should have known when I was nervously interviewed by him. After I left the interview, I felt unusually positive about it.

A few days later, Harold called me at the alternate number I had provided him and offered me the position. I was on cloud nine. My father, uncle and aunt, brother and sister-in-law and the rest of the extended family were happy for my success. It was time to put 1984 behind me and live my own life.

The freedom felt a long time in coming. My struggle with the priesthood call faded into the fire-stained woodwork just as quickly as it had presented itself, never to be pondered again.

"They have everything."

It was the Friday shift before Christmas. I was visiting with my Aunt Donna and my maternal grandmother around the kitchen table before I went to work. My grandmother had always struggled with the commercial aspects of Christmas and the duties of gift giving.

She put so much emphasis on the material side of the gifts that she often imagined that the gifts were unappreciated. Just like her resistance to accepting my brother's wife, Joan, into our family, her Christmas litany of complaints was something Mom and I had often listened to unwillingly, but endured.

"What can I get the kids for Christmas," Grandma Naomi mused. "Surely you can give me ideas."

"Oh I don't know." I always felt put on the spot and never wanted to commit to answering that question, which I hated.

Christmas was supposed to be about family, about being together. This Christmas, I wasn't feeling much in the spirit.

"Well, I always have trouble getting the kids gifts for Christmas, because they have everything."

I had heard this mantra a thousand times before. A thousand times before I let it bounce off and beneath the surface let my emotions simmer.

The imagined "they have everything" idea came from her memories of the great Depression and had nothing to do with our reality now. It was part of my grandmother's own insecurity. It was part of her ritual every Christmas to bemoan my brothers' and sisters' imagined spoiled upbringing.

But this time, the comment came two months after their mother had died and was laid to rest in the Parnell cemetery and one week after the fire.

Have everything?

How in the world could you even think such a thing?

"They don't have everything."

"You don't understand."

"No, it is you who don't understand." The words spilled out of my mouth before I had a moment to catch my breath.

I couldn't sit still and take this any longer. I got up and angrily walked away and left for work without telling anyone goodbye. It was either that or I would say something I would regret forever.

Aunt Donna, unaware of the history of this Christmas ritual that my mother had handled gracefully many times before, was stunned beyond words.

Driving toward Shenendoah with no one to take my anger to did little to calm me down.

I was seeing red.

Logic had gone out of the window. I was driving the vehicle on pure emotion and rage. I thought of all the blessings in our lives, of all the trials of my life, of all the lessons I had learned in my youth, in the military and especially during the past year.

I had to admit to myself that the arrow that had struck my emotional center was fired by my grandmother and I needed faith on this one. I didn't know where to even start looking for it.

"What about everything we've been through?" I screamed to no one in particular, somewhat relieved Grandma Naomi wasn't in my universe at that moment to take in my wrath.

A half-hour into my trip, I slammed on the brakes, thought about my options and then made a totally irrational and emotional decision.

I turned the vehicle around and sped toward my uncle and aunt's house ready to clear this one up once and for all.

Have everything? How dare you.

I was hardly thinking clearly as my detour was going to make me over an hour late to work.

I'm not sure what prompted my grandparents to go home, since so much had been left unsaid and unresolved. Maybe she sensed she had pushed all the wrong buttons and she herself was miffed that I couldn't understand what she was going through.

I truly didn't. I had no idea of the pain she was feeling losing her only daughter. In her eyes she had lost the most valuable thing in the world.

My moment of anger after Mom's death had arrived, part of the grief process. But I had stuffed it in so long that it came out in torrents while I lost total control. No one in the house understood what I was angry at in that moment, but it all came cascading down around my head.

"No, I'm not angry."

You should have been," I screamed in hope that my words would pierce the heavens.

I had seen my grandfather get angry. My grandmother was angry in her own way. And I was now angry.

I couldn't back away from the cliff at the moment.

My brother Norbert stood at the stairwell in awe while he listened to me vent to my father and uncle over things they had no clue about.

As cooler heads prevailed, my father and uncle encouraged me to get to work. I had to call because my side trip was going to make me unfashionably late.

Angry?

"All right, God, yes I am angry," I sighed. "I also don't know if I can find my way back to a relationship with my grandmother."

Driving to work and trying to figure out what I was going to tell my boss, the thought of not being able to reconcile the hurt of my grandmother's arrows scared me even more.

An unlikely messenger

Although I worked the radio board at a Christian radio station, I didn't feel God or the warm fuzziness of faith at the moment. The chill of the anger and unforgiveness of my heart stayed with me throughout the night.

I hated my grandmother at that moment and I saw no way the bridge could be repaired.

God chose to restore me to a reasonable level of sanity in a very unique way. The answers came from my Uncle Joe. We had our own disagreements and not seeing eye to eye through the years, but that Saturday morning he had Solomon's wisdom and was able to get me to see past my own selfish pride and to forgive.

"How would you feel if something happened to her?" he said.

"I know. I'm glad she wasn't here to take my anger, but I just don't know how to find my way back."

"Nobody said it was going to easy," he answered me. "It may take some work. Everyone is under stress. You can't change what happened, but you can change your reaction to it."

Yet I could only take so much, and no, anyone who thought my brothers and sisters had everything, didn't know the losses they had experienced.

That I had experienced.

I couldn't even share my good news about the radio job with my mother. I missed her, and now I had to turn my eyes upward and live my own life. I could no longer hold myself back. It was time to move on.

I didn't realize that was the work God was beginning to manifest in my soul. An unhappiness was setting in, making me uncomfortable in the nest.

Part of my anger stemmed from the fact that it was time for Dad and me to part ways, too, for me to get back to living life. It was time for a new dawn and path in life for all.

Maybe that was why my new job started on January 2nd in the brand new year of 1985, exactly one year after I received that cryptic note in Hobbs, New Mexico about 1984 being a better year for all.

Maybe having a better year was better late than never.

16 - THE PROCESS OF IT ALL

I did my Christmas shopping at Hallmark that year. I spent over an hour looking for the perfect gifts for my grandparents and my father.

I found the comforting words of Helen Steiner Rice fit my mood and idea for Christmas.

I helped my grandmother cut the turkey. I smiled through misty eyes as she shared the stories about Peggy with Grandpa Roy's sister, Mabel, and me.

I was glad that Mabel could stay with my grandparents during their loneliness and grief. Losing her husband, Cleo, a few years back made her the perfect antidote for grieving parents of an adult child.

As gifts were given out, however, the absence of my mother at the event was magnified in everyone's heart. As of yet, we weren't restored to a stable living environment, but the new year would bring some order to chaos.

I wouldn't be totally honest if I tried to claim that everything was all sunshine and no rain from that day forward. I did experience depression and struggled with my new role in life.

However, looking back over 1984, it was a year of miracles. Although I had a definite crisis of faith, God was ever present whether His answers to our prayers were exactly what we wanted or not.

Some of the things that happened after that were that my father remarried in November of 1985, and in January of 1986, I left the career of radio behind and ended up at my hometown newspaper, *The Maryville Daily Forum*, as a general assignment reporter.

The newspaper career would serve me well into the 1990s.

I would marry, have children and, yes, do greater things as Father Regis tried to influence me, even though his goal of molding me as a priest didn't manifest itself.

He did succeed in developing an author, teacher, mentor and counselor.

Father Regis had the hope thing all wrong. Peggy wouldn't let her family give up hope as she herself wasn't about to give up hope. At a critical juncture, when the opportunity for her seven youngest children to see her for the last time presented itself, it was obvious that hope had been extinguished.

She had accepted her fate.

Yes, I needed to let my mother go as the priest encouraged me to do in the St. Francis Hospital corridor—but not that particular day or that particular hour. She was still alive. She was still with us.

Hope is never false when it is grounded in the moment. We have to cherish the blessings of the day, for tomorrow will take care of itself.

My mother's bravery and her battle with cancer would inspire and encourage me when I was faced with a similar challenge in 2010 after I was diagnosed with bladder cancer. Seeing the word "malignant" on the computer screen at the end of my hospital bed made me shiver.

I attribute my survival as I write this to my mother's battle when she taught me it's better to know what you're fighting so you can move against it. Because my mother experienced delays in her treatment, I was quick to advocate for myself and face down the beast with five smooth stones as the David of old did with Goliath.

The result was that I was lucky and God granted me the grace to fell the giant.

My mother had turned two months into nine months—granted, only a few granules of sand in the hourglass, but precious moments to celebrate an anniversary, a birthday and time with special friends and family.

When a person is faced with mortality, priorities shift and changes take place within that soul.

"I don't know what to say."

Then say nothing. Be there. Smile. Show you care.

My call to the priesthood was a red herring for Father Regis. God had no intention of calling me there. However, my call was to be available for my family in 1984.

My Aunt Dee had it right. My radio position in Hobbs, New Mexico didn't work out because it wasn't supposed to. Pulling up stakes and coming home was easy.

What I would discover on my path was a secret older than time itself. Our journey here on earth is brief, but meant to teach us much about ourselves and the world around us.

I know my mother is in heaven looking down on me as I am realizing being creative isn't that much of a burden at all. My hope in the future is that we will one day reunite.

Meanwhile, I have much work waiting for me and I have labored in the fields for many years, accomplishing both small and large things.

God calls each and every one of us according to his purpose, and in 1984 he called me home to help out during my parents' crisis time and need.

If I had it to do it all over again, I would. I have no regrets.

The crucifix that my mother wore on her person throughout her illness is the same crucifix that was in my father's hands after the funeral service.

It is our call to pick up our cross and carry it daily. It will lead us to our own resurrection in Christ, our own truth, our own discovery of our purpose in this life.

It will lead us to tomorrow if we but believe, if we but forgive, if we but learn from what God is trying to tell us through the process of our daily lives.

But around the corner I was to discover even greater truths about grief, about dealing with emotions and loss, about moving on.

God had more for me to learn from the process, and along the way, he blessed me beyond measure for sacrifices made.

My call home in 1984 had been completed; now my life's

work would take me away from home so that my family members could grow and develop into their own unique personas.

I didn't know the fiery furnace of life was to refine and remold my own perceptions of the world and grant me the grace to discover mysteries from my past that would set me free and enhance my understanding of the purpose and power of life.

I believe we all go through a process of "trial by fire," and as my Uncle Joe described, it's not that something has happened, it's what we do with what happened.

I had yet to learn about how the deaths of Elmer and Steve had influenced my life. However, the greatest lesson of all was to experience grief, deal with it, put it away.

My mother wanted to protect Aunt Cecelia and herself by advising Alan and me not to talk about Elmer. It was just too painful. But she had it wrong.

To acknowledge Elmer's existence was to celebrate his brief life, and I learned that I had skipped even the acknowledgement of Steve's death while in boot camp when I should have taken the leave and said goodbye and given support to those he left behind.

Yet, I would have something in common with Steve that God wanted me to understand in my lifetime.

After 1984, I could let go of the responsibility for my family. And in the process, He wanted me to understand the art of forgiveness.

We all struggle. We all stumble. We all strive to make sense of life's events. Sometimes, stuff just happens. We don't always call the shots or make the moves.

A placard I saw recently said, "If God is your co-pilot, switch seats."

When I have humbled myself to do that, I always have found God teaches me something new about myself and gives me wisdom.

In March of 1997, I unwittingly took a route back home that brought me over the river that cost my cousin's life. In that moment, I made a vow to Elmer and Steve to tell their story someday.

The surprise was, the story wasn't the one I thought it would be.

The story was also my mother's story.

Anyone can survive their crisis of faith.
I did.
You can too.
Just look beyond the horizon.

ABOUT THE AUTHOR

Marvin Wilmes resides in Boone, Iowa with his wife, Lori, and children, Wesley and Casey. Marvin is a 1982 graduate of Northwest Missouri State University with a Bachelor of Science degree in Communications. Marvin has worked for newspapers in Maryville, Missouri and Cherokee, Iowa, establishing and operating *The Chronicle* from 1992-97. Marvin began a human services career in 1997 and worked for Woodward Resource Center for the State of Iowa from 1998-2011. Marvin continues to work in human services and customer service and is actively involved in writing his next book.

38077301R00086

Made in the USA
Charleston, SC
31 January 2015